To keep the air pure and the rivers clean, to take some pains to keep the meadows and tillage as pleasant as reasonable use will allow them to be; to allow peaceable citizens freedom to wander where they will, so they do no hurt to garden or cornfield; nay, even to leave here and there some piece of waste or mountain sacredly free from fence or tillage as a memory of man's ruder struggle with nature in his earlier days: is it too much to ask civilisation to be so far thoughtful of man's pleasure and rest, and to help so far as this her children to whom she has most often set such heavy tasks of grinding labour? Surely not an unreasonable asking.

Art under Plutocracy. William Morris (1834-1896) (Morton, 1979)

Acknowledgements

The authors would like to thank all those who responded to our request for comments on the briefing *Green Taxes: pollution payments and labour tax cuts* which we published in June, or who participated in the numerous seminars we have held on aspects of the subject over the past two years. In particular we are grateful to Chris Hewett, Dan Corry and other colleagues at IPPR for help and advice.

This book is part of an EU-wide project on environmental tax reform, set up by David Gee, funded mainly by the European Commission and administered by Chris Hewett at IPPR. We would like to thank the Esmee Fairbairn Foundation, Tesco, NatWest, the Webb Trust and the RSPB for additional financial support, and Cambridge Econometrics for their assistance in kind.

Stephen Tindale is a Senior Research Fellow at IPPR and lecturer in environmental politics at Birkbeck College, University of London. He was previously Secretary to the Labour Party Policy Commission on the Environment.

Gerald Holtham is Director of IPPR and visiting professor at the London Business School. He is a former head of the Economics Division of the OECD.

GREEN TAX REFORM

pollution payments and labour tax cuts

Stephen Tindale
and Gerald Holtham

Contents

Summary

Most people now accept that action must be taken to protect the environment. The British Government has entered into a series of binding international agreements, on global warming, biodiversity, acid rain, ozone depletion and a host of other issues. The opposition parties are in most instances committed to meeting higher targets. As evidence of environmental decline accumulates, pressure for more radical action will grow – the changes currently being discussed or implemented are not nearly enough to make current economic patterns sustainable. This is not an issue which is going to disappear.

The progress which has been made to date has been grudging, rather as if the patient has agreed to give up the favourite tipple only under strict instructions from the doctor. But embracing the environmental agenda should not be seen as a sacrifice. It should be seen, instead, as an opportunity to live a healthier, more fulfilling and more prosperous life. A sustainable economy would not only safeguard the inheritance of our children; it would also improve our economic prospects today. Since the industrial revolution, there has been a dramatic increase in the productivity of labour. Innovation, higher skill levels and new technologies mean that labour productivity will continue to increase. Indeed, at present it appears to be increasing faster than the economy's capacity to create new jobs, and from one cycle to another growing legions are excluded through unemployment. It would surely be sensible to shift some priority onto increasing the productivity with which we use another factor of production, natural resources.

We argue that one of the central tools of environmental policy should be taxation. Green taxes are an effective tool of environmental policy, and that alone is reason enough to introduce them. But they are also an efficient way for governments to raise money, and may even help bolster middle class support for taxation.

The environmental imperative

Chapter One looks at the reasons why governments need to take the environment more seriously. We focus on three issues; there are of course numerous others we could have chosen. Global warming is the greatest environmental challenge of them all, one which will affect everyone. The world is already getting warmer and, according to the international body of scientists set up to advise governments, "current warming trends are unlikely to be entirely natural in origin". Press reports of a recent Department of the Environment study of the likely impact of global warming on the UK have highlighted the improved prospects of the British wine industry. They have not, by and large, focused on the health impacts, the fact that our climate will become wetter as well as warmer, the threat to half of our best agricultural land from rising sea levels. Positive thinking is generally admirable, but this is reminiscent of the optimism of Dr Pangloss.

We do not have to wait for the climate to change to see the impact of pollution on human health. The link between pollution and asthma is now widely understood – whether or not pollution causes the disease, it clearly exacerbates the effects. The link between pollution and cancer is less widely known. According to the Department of Health, several thousand people a year in the UK die prematurely because of pollution. Up to 20,000 more are hospitalised or forced to visit their doctor. This is not only bad for human happiness; it is also bad for the public finances.

The impact of environmental problems is not spread evenly; poor people suffer more. It is a myth that only the middle classes are concerned about the environment. Those living in the East Thames corridor are more affected by pollution than those in the Home Counties. Working class areas are more likely to be targeted for waste disposal facilities. Those with money cannot insulate themselves entirely from the effects of environmental decline, but they can mitigate them. Environmental issues affect everyone, but they do not affect everyone equally. This is one reason why environmentalism must be central to any attempt to redefine social democratic politics.

With so many compelling reasons to take the environment seriously, why does it remain marginalised on the fringes of politics? The answer is that most politicians believe that there is a trade off between environmentalism and their economic objectives. This belief is wrong. There is ample evidence from Britain and abroad that high environmental standards can mean higher levels of economic growth, more employment, higher value-added. But the belief is deep-seated, and is constantly being reinforced by the blandishments of those who gain most from the status quo, the profligates who argue that any interference with their right to do business exactly as they wish will lead to economic stagnation, just as their predecessors argued that the Factory Acts would mark the end of capitalist production. Such special pleading should not be allowed to stand in the way of action.

The case for environmental taxation

In chapter two we consider the form that environmental action should take. We argue that taxation will in many cases be a more efficient way of meeting environmental goals than the alternatives. This is by now a fairly familiar argument, accepted *inter alia* by the OECD, the European Commission and the British government. But the advantages of green taxes go beyond the environmental. By internalising costs which are currently borne by society as a whole, green taxes make the market work better and so enhance economic efficiency, unlike most taxes which distort the economy. And there is considerable public support for the concept of "making the polluter pay", so green taxes which are carefully framed and sensibly implemented (which was manifestly not the case with VAT on fuel) could bolster middle class support for taxation.

We review the use of green taxes in Britain and abroad. There are numerous instruments being used to address a wide variety of problems. Yet the total amount raised from environmental taxes remains low as a proportion of total revenues; less than ten percent in most countries. Chapter three considers why this might be the case by examining the arguments against green taxes. It is sometimes claimed that environmental taxes would need to be prohibitively high to have any significant impact on behaviour. This concern is overstated. Regulation can be used to increase price-responsiveness: an energy tax will be more effective when backed by minimum efficiency standards for buildings and appliances; higher petrol prices will be more effective when combined with sensible land use planning policies; waste taxes will work better if there are also rules on the recycled content of products. The impact will also be increased the longer the taxes are in force.

Will green taxes hurt the poor?

A second objection to green taxes is that they will be regressive. Tax reform which secured environmental or economic improvements at the expense of the poor would rightly be rejected by most people.

The blanket assertion that environmental taxation is regressive greatly oversimplifies the picture. Cuts in government expenditure or a failure to act to protect the environment may be even more regressive. Nevertheless, there are legitimate concerns about the impact of some green taxes, particularly the taxation of domestic energy. The poorest fifth of households spend 12 per cent of their budget on fuel; the richest fifth just four per cent. The poor are less able to cut back on fuel use by changing equipment or installing energy efficiency measures, which can have a high capital cost. And those who live in private rented accommodation have less incentive to invest in insulation since they may not stay long enough to recoup the cost, while the landlords have little incentive because they do not pay the bills.

This suggests that tax should not be used to encourage efficiency in the domestic sector. However, tax measures could be made progressive if the revenue was used to give a lump sum payment to each individual, or possibly to each household. This would be substantially more than the extra tax paid by poorer households, but much less than the extra tax paid by the rich.

Alternative strategies would be to give each household a tax-free fuel allowance, or to spend money insulating the homes of the poor. The latter should certainly be done: it would pay dividends in terms of public health and social justice as well as environmental improvement. It is the appalling state of the British housing stock which makes taxing domestic energy so regressive: these concerns simply do not exist in most other countries. But the work should be done before any tax increase. Otherwise many poor people will be left in the cold while they wait for the extra insulation.

Increasing the cost of motoring is less problematic. This will be a broadly progressive measure over the population as a whole, since very poor people do not own cars – although they may aspire to own them. However, it will be regressive within the car-owning community, impacting more on poor car owners than on rich car owners, and on the rural poor most of all. Some revenue could be used to compensate them, or offsetting tax reductions could be targeted.

It is impossible to say in the abstract whether or not green taxes are regressive. It depends which environmental tax is envisaged, and what will be done with the revenue.

Does environmental protection damage competitiveness?

A further reason why environmental taxation is not more widespread is concern about the impact on international competitiveness. This is often exaggerated. Sudden changes in the cost of, say, energy in one country will have an impact on its ability to compete. The impact of gradual increases, leaving industry time to adapt, may however be positive. Countries with high energy prices, such as Germany and Japan, have tended to be more competitive and wealthier than low-cost nations. This suggests that there is no necessary connection between low energy prices and economic success.

Nevertheless, the impact of tax changes on industrial costs will need to be taken into account, not least for political reasons. No politician is likely, in the current climate, to support measures which lead to a significant increase in the fiscal burden on industry. Does this mean that green taxes for the corporate sector have to be ruled out, or postponed until agreement on co-ordinated action is reached with key competitors? Such agreement will to hard to reach, as the experience of the proposed European carbon/energy tax demonstrates.

Shifting the tax burden

Fortunately there is a way around the difficulty. The revenue from some environmental taxes would need to be spent on specific environment-related purposes: road pricing to fund public transport, for example. But in general it is possible to envisage a shift in the burden of taxation, so that some taxes are reduced as others increase. The overall impact on business could be neutral. Some sectors would experience a decline in competitiveness, but others would find themselves better off.

It is for this reason that attention has focused in recent years on fiscally-neutral tax reform – altering the structure of the tax system without affecting the overall tax burden. This is the subject of chapter four.

Will pollution payments provide a secure revenue stream?

If other taxes are to be reduced and some revenue surrendered, will environmental taxes provide a lasting source of revenue? Many people have dismissed environmental taxes as a revenue source because the more successful they are in reducing pollution, the less revenue the Treasury will receive. Ultimately, if anti-pollution policy is successful, the revenue stream will dry up.

This is again an oversimplification. There is a distinction between activities for which alternatives exist, which may eventually be phased out altogether, and activities which will simply continue at a lower level. An example of the first is the use of chlorine – in Sweden, even a discussion of a tax was enough to prompt industry to phase it out almost completely. In such cases, revenue will not be permanent and so should be used to fund specific programmes. But energy, transport and waste disposal fall into the second category. Revenue from taxes on these activities can therefore be used to fund tax cuts in other areas.

Most sensible proposals for environmental taxes suggest phasing them in gradually. This means that government revenues can be maintained in the face of falling use. Of course, such a process cannot continue without limit. At some point industry will be unable to reduce energy use any further, or it will be prohibitively expensive to do so. Further increases in the rate of taxation would then translate into increased burdens on industry and the substitution of other factors of production for energy. Governments should seek a new equilibrium, at which the economy is operating in a more efficient and ecologically-sustainable manner, with the least possible impact on output, profitability or competitiveness, and the Treasury making some money into the bargain.

There will be errors in predicting the reaction to environmental taxes, and thus how great the revenues will be. But predicting the public finances is hardly an exact science today. There is no reason why revenues from environmental taxation should be any less predictable than those from current taxes.

Should the money be used to fund extra spending?

If a Chancellor decided that higher spending (or lower borrowing) was necessary, environmental taxes would be a good way to raise the money. There may well be a case for increased spending in certain areas (although there is also a case for decreased spending in others). But the argument for increased spending must be kept separate from the debate about how we raise revenue. The point of this report is to argue that a greater proportion of tax revenue should come from environmental taxes. This applies whatever the prevailing level of taxation, spending and borrowing. We therefore argue on the basis of strict tax neutrality: we assume that all the money raised by environmental taxation should be matched by reductions in other taxes.

The "double dividend"

The revenues from environmental taxes could be used to reduce taxes on labour. Across the EU, roughly 50 per cent of all taxes are levied directly or indirectly on labour (mainly through income tax and social security contributions), and less than ten percent on natural resources. The burden of taxation on labour has increased steadily, from around 30 per cent in 1960, while that on natural resources has actually declined.

Tax reform could, it is claimed, deliver a "double dividend" of higher employment and a better environment. The double dividend hypothesis lies behind a series of tax reforms carried out by Northern European countries since 1990. This debate has yet to take off in the UK. There has been considerable discussion about lowering non-wage labour costs – although UK rates of employers' social security contributions are lower than every other European country except Denmark (the highest rates are found in Italy, France and Spain) – less talk of financing cuts in labour taxes by increasing environmental taxes. However, there are encouraging signs. The Government has accepted the principle of environmental tax reform, and the new landfill tax was linked to a reduction in employers' national insurance contributions. The Labour Party commits itself, in its environmental policy document *In Trust for Tomorrow*, to "a long term, gradual change to the way in which the economy is organised, to ensure that it encourages "goods" such as employment, value-added, investment and savings, and discourages "bads" such as pollution and resource depletion". The Liberal Democrats are committed to a unilateral carbon tax, with the revenue used to reduce other taxes.

Options for new green taxes in the UK

Chapter 5 considers which environmental taxes could be increased or introduced. It argues that:

- A new energy tax could be levied on non-domestic users. An energy tax is better than a carbon tax because it will encourage conservation rather than fuel switching.

- Domestic energy taxation should only be increased in conjunction with an "eco-bonus", a proto-basic income which would make the package progressive.

- Road fuel duties could be increased to control the increase in demand for private transport. Diesel should be taxed at the same rate as petrol.

- A "capacity-kilometre tax" to encourage hauliers to use lorry space more efficiently should be considered.

- Company car taxation should be reformed to ensure that it does not encourage people to drive.

- Vehicle Excise Duty could be graded to encourage the purchase of less polluting cars.

- An office parking tax could be introduced to penalise employers who encourage staff to drive to work by providing off-street parking.

- Motorway tolling should only be introduced in conjunction with measures to make the trunk road system less attractive (such as lower speed limits). Revenues could be used to subsidise the rail network.

- Local authorities, including the new London Council, should be given the powers to introduce urban road pricing, and encouraged to experiment.

- The UK should continue to press for global or EU aviation fuel taxes. Failing that, UK airport charges could be increased, and graded according to the weight, engine size or airframe of the planes (which are proxies for pollution).

- The new landfill tax could be increased and extended to incineration. Waste-to-energy plants with the capacity for heat recovery should be exempted.

- Local authorities could be given the power to levy taxes on specific products such as paper plates or packaging for fast food.

- A quarrying tax on primary aggregates could be introduced.

- Charges for water and air pollution should be reformed so that they are related to volume.

- An agricultural input tax could be introduced to discourage the excessive use of fertilisers and pesticides.

A reform package for the UK

The final chapter outlines, for illustrative purposes, a particular package of reforms which could be implemented in the UK. IPPR commissioned Cambridge Econometrics to model a package of difference measures for the period 1997–2005.

Cambridge Econometrics modelled a package of new or increased green taxes and two scenarios for recycling the revenues to preserve tax neutrality. The main elements of the package were:

- a commercial and industrial energy tax

- a waste disposal tax

- a higher road fuel escalator

- a quarrying tax

- reform of company car taxation

- an office parking tax

Two methods of recycling the revenue though lower taxes were modelled:

The Economist's Package: In this scenario all of the revenue is used to reduce employers' NICs. This is the strategy likely to result in the largest overall increase in employment.

The Politician's Package: This scenario recognises that some of the revenue will be needed to win the support of particular groups in society for the reforms. To appeal to the public, ensure that low income households do not lose out and offset some of the increased cost of motoring, the standard rate of VAT is cut. In recognition of the fact that small businesses are less able to react to tax changes by altering behaviour, some of the revenue is used to reduce business rates. The rest is used to reduce employers' NICs.

The reform delivers substantial reductions in emissions of key pollutants. In particular, it delivers a reduction of 9.5 per cent, compared to the base scenario, in total UK carbon emissions in 2005. The main reductions are from road transport (19 per cent), iron and steel (18 per cent), chemicals (12 per cent) and other industry (10 per cent).

There is also a substantial reduction in the amount of waste produced. Total waste disposal falls by 6 per cent in 2000 and 16 per cent in 2005. Landfill is reduced by 18 per cent in 2005.

The main economic impact, as one would expect, is that production has become more job-rich. Under the Economist's Package there are 252,000 extra jobs in 2000, and 717,000 in 2005. Unemployment falls by 300,000; this difference is because not all those who fill the new jobs are registered as unemployed. Two thirds of the new jobs are full-time. All regions gain jobs, though some do better than others. The most significant increases are in health and social work (141,000), business services (91,000), education (61,000) and construction (50,000), but employment in manufacturing industry is also simulated to increase substantially. The impact on other macroeconomic variables is small – again as one would expect with a package which leaves the overall level of taxation unchanged.

The Politician's Package is inferior in job creation terms: it produces 576,000 new jobs rather than 717,000. The impact on GDP, the balance of payments and the RPI remains marginal.

A Green Tax Commission

Those countries which have introduced significant tax reforms along the lines proposed here have prepared the ground by establishing Green Tax Commissions, bringing together politicians (not just from the ruling parties), tax experts, industrialists, environmentalists and trade unionists. We believe that it would be sensible to do the same in the UK. This would ensure that the reforms were sensibly designed and implemented.

However, to ensure that the Commission had sufficient momentum and profile, and did not become bogged down in argument about the principle, it should be given a firm target and timetable. The changes discussed in this paper would involve a tax shift accounting for just under 3 per cent of GDP in 2005. The Commission should be given a year to come up with proposals to shift tax revenues equivalent to 10 per cent of total government revenues onto environmental "bads" within a decade.

1. The environmental imperative

"Action – and action now. The time for looking is past." This call for an environmental crusade came not from Friends of the Earth or Greenpeace, nor even from the Liberal Democrats, but from a Conservative Secretary of State. John Gummer came to the Environment Department with no particular green credentials, but has increasingly been convinced of the need for action by the evidence of environmental decline presented to him by his own advisers. It is time the rest of the political classes took a serious look at this evidence, and responded to the growing public disquiet.

Environmental issues do not rank high in the order of priorities set by a small group of politicians and media editors. We are told every day of the latest fluctuations in the level of the dollar or the Dow Jones, but little about the quality of the air we breathe, the numbers of children admitted to hospital with asthma attacks, the number of new cases of skin cancer. But this tells us more about the attitude of an elite than it does about the concerns of the public. For millions of people, the day-to-day reality of polluted air and water, the loss of ever-more countryside, are more real and more significant than the latest statistics on the balance of trade or the prospects of a European single currency. The increasing membership of environmental groups, the demonstrations and protests in defence of threatened sites, the high level of environmental awareness among young people; all are evidence of growing concern. Opinion polls confirm the impression: a Mori poll for *The Times* in July 1996 found that more people were concerned about the environment than about the future of the EU.

The reasons for this concern are myriad, and not hard to understand. From the global threats of climate change and ozone depletion to local issues such as urban air quality or nature conservation, the picture is one of increasing environmental pressures being met with inadequate political response. The gulf between the enormity of the problems and the paucity of the proffered solutions remains striking, and depressing.

The reasons why governments should pay more attention to environmental issues could fill a whole book – indeed they have filled many excellent books. We will focus on just three: climate change, the impact of pollution on health, and environmental justice.

Climate change

There is now a remarkable degree of consensus about global warming. No one doubts that a scientific phenomenon, known as the Greenhouse Effect, traps some of the heat from the sun in the Earth's atmosphere. Without it, life would be impossible. No one doubts either that atmospheric concentrations of carbon dioxide and other greenhouse gases have increased dramatically since the pre-industrial age, and are continuing to rise.

The question is whether increased concentrations of these gases will enhance the Greenhouse Effect, leading to climate change. This possibility has been under consideration by scientists for exactly a century; it was first identified in 1896 by the Swedish chemist Svante Arrhenius. It is thus neither new nor a fad. But given the magnitude of the challenge, governments felt it prudent to try to clarify the scientific thinking. They therefore created the Intergovernmental Panel on Climate Change (IPCC). This produced its first report in 1990, a second in 1992, and yet another in 1995. The last of these involved the work of 899 leading international scientists. Noting that over the past century global mean temperature has increased by 0.3–0.6 degrees centigrade, the IPCC concluded that current warming trends are "unlikely to be entirely natural in origin" and that "the balance of evidence suggests that there is a discernible human influence on global climate".

There can be few topics which have been scrutinised so thoroughly, and on which such a broad consensus can be forged. Yet still governments plead "uncertainty" as an excuse to postpone decisions. Of course it is still possible to find a small number of scientists why deny that climate change will happen, just as it is possible to find people who deny the link between HIV and AIDS. Fortunately public health programmes to prevent the spread of HIV were not delayed until this small band of irreconcilables was convinced. Many (though not all) of the remaining sceptics are scientists carrying out work commissioned and paid for by the oil industry. When a tobacco company argues that the dangers of passive smoking are exaggerated, its claims are rightly greeted with ridicule. When an oil company argues that the dangers of global warming are exaggerated, its claims are treated as a serious contribution to the debate, and a welcome excuse for postponing action.

Governments are able to get away with continuing procrastination by confusing, deliberately or otherwise, the fact of global warming with the effects it will have. While the former is established, and indeed underway, the exact impacts remain uncertain. This is hardly surprising given the timescales involved and the complexity of the mechanisms. The impact will be different in different parts of the world, and feedback mechanisms such as cloud formation or local pollution levels will alter the overall pattern. General predictions can be made: according to IPCC average global temperatures will increase by between 1.5 degrees centigrade and 3.5 degrees (the last Ice Age was only five degrees centigrade colder than today); sea levels will rise, probably by around 50 cm but possibly as much as 95 cm, inundating low lying areas; there will be an increase in extreme weather conditions and "natural" disasters, including floods and droughts. Agriculture in the developing world will be particularly hard hit. All of this will mean an increase in the number of environmental refugees seeking to escape to the developed world.

Some effects of global warming are already evident: for example, in the Arctic, the rate at which the ice melts has increased from 2.5 per cent per decade to 4.3 per cent, while in the Antarctic two ice shelves, which a 1970s climate model predicted would be the first to disappear as warming took hold, have recently collapsed. But the full impacts will not be known until they occur.

If the effects are uncertain, would it perhaps be prudent to wait until they are clearer before taking action, as recommended, for example, by that bastion of common sense, *The Economist*? It would not, for several reasons. First, the policies which are needed – energy efficiency, rational transport policies, reforestation – would be sensible even without the Greenhouse Effect, and many of them would even be good for the economy. Secondly, the effects may not manifest themselves in convenient, gradual and manageable ways, leaving us time to adjust. Third, the warming that has already occurred is exacerbating other environmental threats which we face. For example, the 1996 ozone hole over the Northern hemisphere was the worst ever – levels over the UK in February were only just over half normal levels for that time of year. This was the third winter out of four in which a deep Arctic hole has formed. The stratosphere was colder than normal, thus facilitating ozone destruction, because more heat was being trapped in the lower atmosphere by global warming.

Global warming is also implicated in the dramatic increase in what we used to term "natural" disasters or "acts of God". The damage wrought by storms, floods, hurricanes and so on is spiralling upward. In the first three years of the 1990s, there were twice as many major windstorms world-wide as in the whole of the 1980s, causing damage worth $20 billion. This is why the insurance industry is taking global warming so seriously. The major companies all have global warming units, and lined up with environmentalists in pushing for greater action at the latest session of international negotiations on the Climate Change Convention. A publication entitled *Global Warming: element of risk*, published by the reinsurance company Swiss Re, sums up the concern:

> This hazard has to be contained rather than intensified. And the damage which can no longer be prevented should at least be limited. We have to rethink, correct our mistakes and win time. Instead, public discussion still centres on whether the problem exists at all. And if it does, whether there is any need to react. The answer given by climatologists leaves no doubt whatsoever. We do indeed have a problem, and it is far more serious than would appear at first glance.

Whatever surprises global warming has in store for us, it is unlikely that many of them will be pleasant, and the more that can be avoided the better. A recent DoE report (DoE 1996a) highlighted some of the potential effects of climate change on the UK. By 2050 sea levels could rise by 35 cm, increasing the risk of storm surge damage, flooding and salinity. Over 50 per cent of the grade 1 agricultural land in England and Wales could be affected. The frequency of gales will increase by 30 per cent, with consequent damage to property and agriculture.

Steep reductions in greenhouse gas emissions are necessary to mitigate the impact, to prevent serious disruption of weather patterns and agriculture, and to avoid a scenario in which millions of environmental refugees are forced to flee floods, drought and famine. The EU Ministerial Statement at the 1996 conference on the Climate Change Convention accepted that cuts of 50 per cent of carbon dioxide emissions will be needed to stabilise atmospheric concentrations. Without significant policy changes, emissions will rise substantially – according to the International Energy Agency, energy consumption in the OECD countries alone will increase by about 30 per cent in the next fifteen years if policy remains unchanged. (IEA, 1994)

In the UK, all three major political parties have recognised the threat of global warming, and are pledged to take action, though none faces up to the scale of the challenge. The Government has promised reductions in Greenhouse Gas emissions of five to ten per cent (from 1990 levels) by

2010. Labour has promised a 20 per cent reduction by 2010. The Liberal Democrats promise cuts of two per cent a year. It is becoming increasingly probable that the international community will agree significant cuts under the Climate Change Convention. In July 1996 the US government, previously opposed to binding commitments, announced a change of heart; with its under Secretary for Global Affairs stating: "let me make clear the US view: the science calls upon us to take urgent action; the IPCC report is the best science we have and we should use it".

Illness and the environment

A second reason why we need to take the environment more seriously is that current levels of pollution are bad for our health. All major political parties talk of the importance of a preventative health strategy. Yet health policy remains stuck in a mindset which concentrates on treating people once they fall ill rather than ensuring that they remain healthy. This is bad for human happiness – much avoidable pain and suffering has to be endured as a result. It is also bad economics. Britain spends around £30 billion a year on the NHS, and governments boast of how they have increased expenditure. Yet health spending is in many respects an indication of failure: the failure to protect public health. And one of the main threats to public health is pollution. As an article in the *British Medical Journal* noted in 1992:

> Doctors seem to spend their time these days exhorting their patients to adopt healthier habits: to exercise more, eat less, drink only a little, smoke not at all; to wear seat belts, crash helmets, and condoms. But perhaps the most important risks to health are beyond people's immediate control, caused by the unhealthy habits not of individuals but of an energy hungry and throwaway society"
>
> (Godlee and Walker, 1992)

One in seven British children now suffers from asthma. Medical consensus appears to be that the epidemic is caused by allergens in the home, but that pollution exacerbates the effects, bringing on attacks. Hospital admissions for asthma go up during air pollution episodes.

The Department of the Environment has recently published an air quality strategy, which represents a clear acceptance of the link between air pollution and health. It cites a Department of Health assessment that pollution causes several thousand advanced deaths each year, along with 10–20,000 hospital admissions and "many thousands" of cases of illness, reduced activity, distress and discomfort (DoE, 1996b).

The key air pollutants and their impact on health are:

- **Nitrogen oxides (NO$_x$)**; NO$_x$ are among the gases which trigger asthma attacks, and increase susceptibility to infections. High levels are lethal – an episode in London in December 1991 is estimated to have killed 160 people. NO$_x$ gases also react with other pollutants to form low-level ozone (see below). Half of total UK emissions come from road transport, a quarter from power stations, most of the rest from industry.

- **Sulphur dioxide**; released by burning fossil fuels which contain sulphur, particularly coal. Health affects are mainly respiratory, and at high levels can be lethal. A recent study published in the Journal of Epidemiology and Community Health (1996) reported that the death rate in Athens jumps by 12 per cent when sulphur dioxide levels are high. Two-third of UK emissions come from power stations, the rest mainly from industry.

- **Carbon monoxide**; a threat to those with cardio-vascular problems. Over 90 per cent of total UK emissions are from road transport.

- **Particulates**; small particles of soot, emitted mainly from vehicles (and more from diesel than petrol). Small particulates are inhaled deep into the lung, often carrying carcinogenic hydrocarbons coated to their surface. One reputable estimate, in the journal *Nature*, suggests that 10,000 people die prematurely in the UK every year as a result of small particulates (known as PM10s) in diesel fumes – roughly equivalent to one major aircrash every fortnight. The Government has accepted that there is a causal link between levels of small particulates and mortality and morbidity. (DoE 1996b). Particulates are also implicated in asthma. Over half of UK particulate emissions come from road transport, and pollution from this source is still rising.

- **Hydrocarbons/Volatile Organic Compounds (VOCs)**; released from a wide range of sources. Some are respiratory irritants, others are carcinogens. One which has caused significant concern in recent years is benzene. The WHO states that there is no safe level of exposure; human beings run an increased risk of cancer even with the smallest dose.

- **Ground-level ozone**; produced by a chemical reaction involving NO$_x$, VOCs and sunlight. Ozone cuts out harmful ultraviolet rays – this is why it is essential in the stratosphere – but at ground level there is concern about its toxicity, which impairs respiratory functions, leading to chronic or acute reduction in lung function, exacerbation of pre-existing lung diseases, increased risk of infection, acquisition of allergic sensitivity and impairment of lung development.

The Government is setting a series of targets to reduce these and other pollutants by 2005 as part of its air quality strategy – mandated by the 1995 Environment Act. But the policy instruments to meet the targets are, in many instances, not in place. For example, the new target for nitrogen dioxide will require reductions at kerbside locations by up to 70 per cent (from 1995 levels). The EU's post-2000 vehicle standards will deliver reductions of, at most, 47 per cent, leaving what the DoE admits is "a clear policy gap". Post-2000 vehicle and fuel standards agreed by the EU will reduce particulate emissions by around half, but much greater reductions are needed to protect public health.

The potential health impact of climate change could also be severe, and provides further reason not to delay in tackling the problem. As Sir Donald Acheson, former Chief Medical Officer, writes: "the potential risks to health, indeed to survival itself, for many millions of people are so dire that 'as with acute medical emergencies, there is no time to wait for the return of the investigations which could confirm the diagnosis'" (Godlee and Walker, 1992).

Ozone formation at ground level is expected to increase as a result of global warming. In the longer term, according to the DoE's Climate Change Impacts Review Group, there will be an increase in the number of insects in the UK, with consequent increases in the risk of vector-borne diseases such as encephalitis (brain inflammation), leishmaniasis (a disease transmitted by sandflies which is already endemic in most of Portugal, Spain, Italy and Greece) and malaria – though they believe that public health measures should suffice to control the latter. There will be an increase in heat-related deaths, although this will be partially offset by a decrease in cold-related deaths. Changes is the frequency and severity of extreme weather events will have both direct and indirect health impacts. Overall they conclude that "it is a prudent assumption that climate change would, on balance, constitute a serious long-term hazard to human health" (DoE 1996a).

Environmental justice

A third compelling reason to face up to the environmental challenge is that current levels and patterns of environmental degradation are inequitable.

"Environmental, social and physical stresses are all generally more severe in the poorest section of the community" (Crombie, 1994). Inner-city residents suffer more from transport-related pollution, and in the UK this generally means poorer people; the more affluent have long since fled to the greener and less polluted suburbs. (Indeed the reason why London's West End is fashionable and East End is not is that the prevailing winds blow the pollution from the West to the East.) Working class communities are less adept at lobbying against undesirable environmental developments being located in their "backyards" – in the USA the Environmental Justice Movement has mapped how almost all toxic tips are located in poor neighbourhoods, particularly those where most residents are from ethnic minorities. And poor people will be less able to protect themselves from the health effects of environmental decline. To take one example: ozone depletion will lead to more eye problems as more UV radiation gets through the protective screen in the stratosphere. When Margaret Thatcher had an eye problem she was taken straight into a private hospital and emerged, one day and one operation later, recovered. How many of the tens of thousands of predicted cataract cases in Africa will be so lucky?

Global warming will impact more heavily on the developing world than on the rich "North". Agriculture in the tropics will be more seriously affected than agriculture in temperate zones. Drought and desertification will make some areas uninhabitable; other areas will be flooded. A low-lying country like the Netherlands will be better able to adjust than similar but poorer countries like Bangladesh, Egypt or the Maldives. Those who welcome the prospect of a Mediterranean climate in Britain (and who generally ignore the fact that Britain will probably be wetter as well as warmer), should be aware that the actual Mediterranean will be suffering from chronic droughts, and that river deltas which are home to millions of people will have disappeared beneath the waves. If this does not bother them, perhaps the likely fate of Venice will.

Tony Crosland, when he was Labour's Environment Secretary, railed against the selfishness of middle class environmentalists who wanted to "pull the ladder up behind them" by stopping some developments or restricting the growth of car ownership and use. This was characteristically bombastic, and uncharacteristically wrong. There are, of course, the infamous NIMBYs, but the great majority of environmentalists are more generous in spirit and more sophisticated than Crosland allowed, recognising that it is the poor who suffer most from environmental degradation. Environmental issues affect everyone, it is often claimed. This is true, but it does not mean that they affect everyone equally.

Economic and environmental needs

It might be argued that what poor people really care about are the classic "pocket book issues" in particular unemployment. They might regard cleaner air as nice, but not as nice as a job or more money. Environmental improvements, on this view, will have to be postponed until we have got the economy right.

Progressive politicians are right to place joblessness at the top of their agenda. For if environmental decline is a pervasive and chronic crisis, unemployment is an immediate and acute one. Society is in danger of tolerating the intolerable: persistent levels of unemployment which leave millions without work, families worn out by poverty, communities without hope and vulnerable to crime. A sense of fatalism is setting in; the full employment of the 1950s and 1960s is seen as a historical aberration, not a norm to which we can return. The failure to reduce unemployment is the central reason why democratic politics is everywhere falling into disrepute. No progressive government worthy of the name can duck the challenge of full employment.

But this does not mean that environmental progress should be postponed. The child suffering from bronchial disease caused by polluted air should not be made to wait for full employment before getting relief. And fortunately we do not have to make this choice. The view that the goals of environmental protection are opposed to the goals of economic expansion has been allowed to persist for far too long. Of course there is a tension between some forms of economic activity – nuclear power or chlorine manufacture, for example – and the need to protect our environment. A responsible government would try to minimise or phase out these activities. But there is no general conflict between economic and environmental goals.

It is not the fact of economic activity which damages the environment, but the particular pattern of economic activity which has developed since the industrial revolution. Much of the reform needed to make the economy more sustainable, such as investment in cleaner technologies and action to insulate homes and offices, will itself increase economic growth. This will go with the grain of economic trends: information-based or service industries tend to have a much lower environmental impact than manufacturing. The question of growth is in fact irrelevant: it all depends what is growing.

Since the industrial revolution, world energy use has increased dramatically:

total energy consumption has increased seventy-fold since 1860 (when the increase in consumption was already well underway); global annual coal consumption is a hundred times greater than it was in 1800; oil consumption is 250 times higher than in the late nineteenth century (Ponting, 1991). To a certain extent this is inevitable – urbanised industrial societies will always consume more energy than rural, agricultural ones. But beyond a certain point, the link between economic development and energy use breaks down. The most advanced economies, such as the Japanese, have successfully decoupled increased economic activity from increased energy use; they now require less energy per unit of GDP. This is a key measure of environmental productivity; the amount of wealth or well-being derived from every unit of natural resource used. Since the industrial revolution, there has been a twenty-fold increase in the productivity of labour. Yet global energy productivity did not begin to increase, on average, until 1973 (Von Weizacker, 1994). If future increases in efficiency are not to be bought at a cost of ever-increasing unemployment coupled with longer and harder work for those with jobs, we need to focus now on securing similar increases in environmental productivity. On the Government's own figures, British industry could reduce its energy use by 20 per cent, with no loss of output, by investing in energy-efficiency measures which would be cost-effective even at today's energy prices (DoE 1994). Companies do not do so because it is simply not high enough up the corporate agenda, and many managers are not aware of the scope for increased efficiency.

Governments can encourage sustainable activity by supporting the industries of the future: high-tech, high-skill, high value-added industries which have low environmental impacts. One important growth sector is environmental industry: pollution abatement equipment such as catalytic converters for cars or scrubbers for power stations, and clean technologies which include redesigned processes to ensure that less energy is used and less waste produced. The market for environmental industries is already enormous. According to OECD calculations, for pollution abatement alone the global market is $250 billion, and will be worth over $300 billion by the end of the decade, which is more than the global aerospace market. The market for clean technologies will be even bigger. At the moment Germany, Japan and the USA are leading in environmental exports, and in all three countries the private sector is actively supported by the government. The US government provided $4 billion in support in 1994; Germany, Japan and the USA all provide tax incentives for investment in clean technology or pollution abatement equipment. Perhaps most importantly, the three leaders all have high environmental standards at home, giving their industries a strong base from which to expand. Failure to adopt high standards in Britain has left our industries at a competitive disadvantage. Sensible environmental regulations encourage innovation and investment which make companies more productive and less wasteful, and thus better able to compete.

Developing environmental industries and services would be a way to create new jobs to replace those lost in declining sectors. In the German *Land* of North Rhine Westphalia, for example, around 770,000 jobs were lost in mining and heavy industry between 1984 and 1994. But in the same period over 800,000 new jobs were created by investing in conservation and recycling industries and other services. This is not surprising: recycling is more labour-intensive than waste disposal; energy conservation is more labour-intensive than power generation.

Diverting public spending away from damaging options towards more environmental ones could also result in a net gain in jobs. Building railways is much more labour-intensive than building roads. Sustainable agriculture would mean more people working on the land. And if any extra money is available – for example from a windfall tax – a programme of environmental restoration would be a worthwhile and labour-intensive way of spending it.

Far from there being a conflict between jobs and the environment, then, high standards and a vigorous environmental policy would help move society back towards full employment, and are needed to ensure that a country develops industries appropriate for the next century. By neglecting the green agenda, politicians not only miss the chance to improve public health and restore the environment; they are also letting down the unemployed. Put another way: the environment is not something to worry about once we have solved our economic problems; it is part of the solution to our economic problems.

This point is central to the perennial debate about whether a country such as Britain should act alone, or whether it should wait for multilateral action. Britain is responsible for less than three per cent of global Greenhouse Gas emissions, and while there might be some scope to influence others by the force of example, there would be little point in inflicting economic damage upon ourselves if others continued to pollute. If unilateral action did involve economic sacrifices this would be a tricky debate involving complex cost-benefit analysis. As it is, we can spare ourselves much of the agonising. Co-ordinated global or European action is desirable. but in its absence, Britain should act alone. We have little to lose, and much – a healthier population, a more efficient economy, even some enhanced respect in the population, a more efficient economy, even some enhanced respect in the international community – to gain. The problems are global, but the solutions can be national.

Vested interests

If the environmental agenda is such a positive, problem-free affair, one has to wonder why British politicians have been so wary of it. In essence, the answer is that there are powerful interests who oppose any change in the pattern of economic behaviour. The fossil fuel and chemical industries are alert to the dangers to their interests posed by environmental concerns; their lobbying operations are well-resourced, well-organised and not overly-principled. This is what John Gummer was referring to in his speech to the Climate Change Conference in July 1996 when he attacked "the purveyors of falsehood who put their selfish concerns before the interests of the world community" and counselled that "none of us should give way to the commercial propositions which are hidden by the pseudo-science of those who pretend that what the world knows to be true can be put on one side because of an individual's desire to promote his particular and prejudiced view". When a Conservative Cabinet Minister talks about big business in this way, one can safely assume that there is some serious special pleading going on behind the scenes.

Trade unions have historically campaigned to protect existing jobs, rather than supporting reforms which might lead to higher levels of employment overall, but would involve job losses in some sectors. Nuclear power is the classic example – it is both capital-intensive and expensive, but has been supported by unions for its employment generation, largely because nuclear facilities are located in areas where alternative employment options are currently limited. Fortunately there are signs of change in the trade union attitude. For example, MSF has been campaigning for many years for government policies to promote clean technologies, recognising that this could create thousands of jobs, and arguing that "environmental diversification" should be an essential part of any industrial strategy; UNISON has sponsored research into the employment-creation potential of environmental policy.

In general, however, those lobbying for change tend to be far less powerful than those supporting business as usual. Many of the industries they wish to promote are either small or not yet in existence, so are not very helpful in fund-raising terms. Britain now has an Environmental Industries Commission, which does useful work. But it cannot compete with the big

Environmental groups, many of which now campaign by offering solutions rather than simply highlighting problems, represent the strongest lobby for change. Their success has led to an inevitable backlash, with some writers claiming that they sensationalise and distort the facts in order to attract attention. Environmental groups are not saintly paragons. They make mistakes. They sometimes do exaggerate or sensationalise (though trying to get anyone to take notice without doing one of these is a tall order). There are legitimate questions to be asked about their accountability. But it should be recognised that their overall contribution is positive, indeed essential, since British political parties have proved inadequate in the field of environmental protection. They are interest groups, but the interest they represent is the public one. Nobody chooses a career as an environmentalist in order to get rich (although there is a modicum of fame to be had when things are going well). Greenpeace has no financial interest in seeing higher environmental standards adopted – indeed the amelioration of some of the more visible problems would lead to a drop in income.

The main problem with environmental groups is not that they are self-interested, but that they are under-resourced. They generally have to rely not on their own science or analysis, but on the pronouncements of others, in particular government agencies. Indeed one of the ironies of environmental politics is that one often finds NGOs furiously lobbying governments to take note of the governments' own advisers. This is an essential part of pressure politics – governments are forced by public concern into setting up enquiries or advisory bodies, but have to be forced once again to take note of what they say. The Intergovernmental Panel on Climate Change is perhaps the best example of this, but there have been similar chains of events regarding urban air quality, acid rain and habitat loss.

This report uses the same approach: wherever possible we use official publications to back up our arguments – be it on the seriousness of the environmental crisis or the benefits of green taxes. What is needed is not for governments to accept the environmentalists' case uncritically, but for politicians to listen to the advice of the very scientists and other experts who they have appointed to advise on particular matters – and to resist the blandishments of vested interests who seek to persuade them that these were the wrong scientists addressing the wrong issues. The environmental agenda requires imagination and boldness, a willingness to consider the evidence and, where it is convincing, act upon it, even where this means standing up to powerful lobbies. Politicians need to display some leadership. This is, after all, what we pay them for.

How should we act?

This chapter has argued that environmental action is essential. For those convinced by the argument, the next questions is: what sort of action? The next chapter will argue that taxation is in many cases an appropriate, efficient and effective way to protect the environment. It is not the only way; it will not be suitable or acceptable in all cases, and will almost always work best in combination with regulations and educational campaigns. But taxation to make prices reflect the full social and environmental cost of particular activities is a necessary part of a transition to a sustainable society.

This is not to say that environmental taxation is problem free. Anyone who thought this will have been disabused of the notion by the cack-handed imposition of VAT on domestic fuel. Nevertheless, there is reason to believe that green taxes which are carefully framed and sensibly implemented (neither of which was the case in that instance) can help in tackling a parallel crisis – the loss of public support for taxation. The widely-accepted notion of making the polluter pay could mean that green taxes enjoy greater legitimacy and public tolerance than other taxes. Moreover, environmental taxation is an efficient way to raise money. Whereas most taxes distort economic activity, green taxes can make the market work better.

There are thus three arguments for green taxes: an fiscal one, a political one and an environmental one. These are considered in the next chapter.

2. Environmental taxation

A properly functioning tax system should raise revenue in the least distorting way – doing the least possible damage to economic activity and incentives. It should reflect popular conceptions of fairness. It should be clearly linked to accountable democratic structures. And it should encourage features of economic activity which society wishes to encourage – such as employment, value added, profit and saving – while discouraging aspects which need to be reduced, like resource use, pollution or waste.

These objectives may conflict. It is not easy to design a fiscal system which meets all of them in all respects. The case for reform rests on the fact that most existing fiscal systems fail to meet most of them. They send the wrong signals to economic actors, raise revenue through highly distorting and often regressive taxes, and fail to command public support. This gives an opportunity to move the environment to the centre of the political stage. Green taxes could help overcome the fiscal crisis which threatens all welfare capitalist states.

The fiscal case for green taxes

Economic theory suggests that most taxes are distortionary to a greater or lesser extent. Taxes change relative prices, generally raising the work time needed to buy goods, so creating disincentives for production and work. While taxes will often reallocate or redistribute resources in a desirable way, there is generally some deadweight loss involved.

However, not all taxes are distortionary. Market prices do not always reflect the full cost of an activity, and in such cases taxes can enhance efficiency. Some of the costs, of pollution for example, are not borne by the producer but dispersed on to society. The producer therefore does not need to charge for them, and so produces more pollution than is optimal. Environmental taxes or pollution payments encourage firms and individuals to use resources more efficiently and thus help to maximise welfare.

A firm buys oil from an oil company to power its factory. The market price is set by the oil company, on the basis of the costs of extraction, refining and distribution, its need to satisfy its shareholders and the price being offered by its competitors. This is a straightforward transaction between two economic actors. However, when the oil is used the factory emits pollution which damages the health of those living nearby. They suffer a loss of amenity, and the state has to pay for their healthcare. This is not reflected in the price of oil. If an oil tax is introduced, the state recoups its costs from the factory. The factory then finds oil more expensive. so uses it more efficiently. This reduces the state's revenue, but also its costs, since less pollution is emitted and the population remains healthier.

The impact of pollution on those living near the factory is a classic example on an environmental "externality". The theoretical work prescribing taxation to internalise externalities was pioneered by the British economist Arthur Cecil Pigou in books such as *Wealth and Welfare* (1912) and *Economics of Welfare* (1920). The most famous example Pigou uses of an externality is the spark from a steam engine which sets fire to a surrounding wood and causes economic damage. He also refers to pollution problems and the economic impact of the then-notorious urban smogs. He quotes from a 1918 study in Manchester which proved an annual loss of £290,000 in terms of extra laundry costs, artificial light and damage to buildings as a result of heavy pollution (Pigou, 1920).

By internalising external costs, environmental taxes encourage economic actors to use resources more efficiently and so help to maximise welfare. So unlike most taxes, which damage economic efficiency, environmental taxes can actually improve it. Kenneth Clarke accepted this argument in his 1994 Budget speech: "in some cases, taxes actually do some good, by helping markets work better and by discouraging harmful or wasteful activity". Putting this point another way, economic actors do not currently pay the full price of their actions; the shortfall is covered from the public purse. They are therefore receiving an implicit subsidy to pollute. Removing this subsidy would encourage individuals and firms to take responsibility for their decisions, which would then be based on full and accurate information. It would also save public money – revenue foregone through an implicit subsidy has the same effect on the PSBR as revenue disbursed through actual subsidy. The Treasury has recognised that "failure or inability to charge for external costs or to ensure appropriate regulation may result in an implicit subsidy". But it displays an unusually cavalier attitude to the scope and extent of these subsidies, and does not appear to have a comprehensive analysis of their extent. (Treasury, 1996).

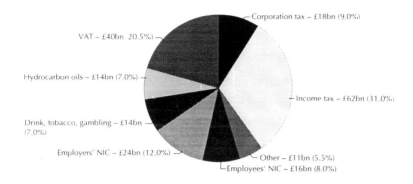

Fig. 2.1: How the taxman gets his money (1994 figures)

One could conclude, as the European Commission has, that "in financing government expenditure, the taxman should rely heavily on environmental taxation" (European Commission, 1993a). Yet European governments raise less than ten per cent of their revenue from environmental taxes, compared with over half from various taxes on labour. The UK conforms to this picture, as the above chart shows.

Taxes need to be simple and cost-effective to administer, and difficult to evade. One of the many failings of the poll tax was the cost and difficulty of collection. Rates were attached to buildings, which tend not to move about or disappear. The poll tax attached to individuals, who do both. Taxes which have theoretical attractions but which impose significant burdens on either the public authorities or the liable parties are unlikely to find favour. Green taxes could be designed to be easy to administer: the Swedish Government reports that the administration costs of its carbon dioxide tax, introduced in 1991, are "low in relation to other indirect taxation, and much lower than, for example, tax on income" (Swedish Ministry of the Environment, 1995).

The political case for green taxes

Green taxes, then, are an efficient way for governments to raise revenue. A further attraction is that they may, if carefully designed and implemented, be less unpopular than other taxes. This statement is likely to raise a hollow laugh among British politicians, who consider that VAT on fuel has destroyed this argument once and for all. But this view is mistaken. VAT on fuel was rightly unpopular, as will be seen from the discussion in the next chapter. But the fact that it is possible to have unpopular environmental taxes does not mean that all environmental taxes must be unpopular.

There are some grounds for believing that environmental taxes may be more acceptable to voters than income taxes. The 1992 British Social Attitudes Report records that 60 per cent of respondents agreed with the statement "the Government should do more to protect the environment, even if it leads to higher taxes". Only 11 per cent disagreed. Sixty-seven per cent supported the statement that "ordinary people should do more to protect the environment, even if it means paying higher prices", once again 11 per cent disagreed (British Social Attitudes, 1992). Of course this has to be taken with more than a pinch of salt. As politicians of the Left have found to their cost, many people will tell opinion pollsters that they are prepared to pay higher taxes, then use the secrecy of the polling booth to vote for the party offering to lower them. However, if one is talking not about higher taxes but about different taxes, the evidence may be more reliable. And it is easy to see why environmental taxation might appeal more than income taxes: the former is a tax on behaviour generally accepted to be "bad" in some sense (pollution, waste, resource depletion), while the latter is "a tax on the hard-earned rewards of ordinary people". The widespread acceptance of high taxes on alcohol and cigarettes is an example of the consensus which can be forged on fiscal matters.

"Making the polluter pay" should therefore be used as one of the principles of a modern tax system. This does not mean that it will be the only principle, or even the paramount one. Public support for other principles – notably for the concept of fair taxes – remains encouragingly strong. Tax policy needs to balance different principles, a lesson Lamont forgot when he introduced a highly-regressive green tax. But recognising these constraints, one can still conclude that environmental taxes have an important role to play in bolstering middle class support for taxation. This would be a significant contribution to political life: as FD Roosevelt pointed out, taxes are the dues we pay for the privilege of living in a civilised society.

The environmental case for green taxes

The main reason for introducing new or increased green taxes, however, is environmental. Green taxes are necessary because without them, finite resources are squandered and unnecessary pollution and waste are produced.

Taxation will, in many cases, be the most efficient way to meet environmental goals. A tax will encourage those companies who can alter their behaviour most easily and cheaply to do so, while those for whom adjustment would be expensive will simply pay the tax. Pollution will thus be reduced at least cost to society. A regulatory approach, which required all companies to alter behaviour equally, would be less efficient. This general point is now widely accepted. For example, the European Union's latest action programme on the environment promises to make much wider use of "market mechanisms".

The arguments for taxes rather than regulation came to prominence with a minority report from the Royal Commission on Environmental Pollution in 1972, signed by the Oxford Economist Wilfred Beckerman and the scientist Lord Zuckerman, which urged the Government to introduce pollution charges. Beckerman subsequently outlined his arguments in a paper for the Institute of Economic Affairs (Beckerman, 1975). The deregulatory claims of Beckerman's case have obvious rhetorical appeal to those committed to "roll back the frontiers of the state" – even though in effect a tax is as much an interference in free market operations as a regulation is. The argument also appealed to the New Right belief that the burden of taxation should shift from direct to indirect taxes, which are seen as more compatible with individual freedom, even if the expenditure is essential and thus involuntary.

The right wing think tanks retained an interest in market mechanisms for environmental protection through the 1980s and early 1990s (eg Taylor, 1992). More recently they have tended more towards papers questioning the validity of environmental concern and so opposing any form of government activity, fiscal or regulatory. (eg Bate and Morris, 1994) This position is at least intellectually coherent, although it demands a degree of myopia not often found outside the new Right. It is helpful in that it destroys the myth that environment taxation is somehow a right-wing instrument and regulation a left-wing one.

The intellectual case for market mechanisms was given a boost in 1989 by the publication of a Government-sponsored report called *Blueprint for a Green Economy*, by a group of academics led by David Pearce of University College, London. Pearce and his colleagues argued, first, that "business as usual" was not a sustainable proposition; second, that taxes were a more efficient means of changing behaviour than regulation; and third (and more controversially) that the proper level of such taxes could be calculated by placing a monetary value on environmental quality.

Blueprint was widely acclaimed and even more widely debated. The 1990 White Paper on the Environment, *This Common Inheritance*, stated that:

Regulation [has] limitations. It can be expensive to monitor and difficult to update quickly in response to scientific and technical advance. It cannot always pitch controls at the level which strikes the most effective balance between environmental benefits and compliance costs... Regulation has always been required and is still required, but it has its shortcomings. For these reasons the Government, along with other governments throughout the world, has begun to look for ways to control pollution which avoid some of these problems by working with the grain of the market (DoE 1990).

Blueprint also succeeded in focusing the minds of the Opposition and the environmental movement on green taxes. So too did a 1990 publication from the Institute for Fiscal Studies (Pearson and Smith, 1990) which again argued the superiority of taxes over regulation. The Labour Party, in schizophrenic mode, halfway between its command economy phase and the market enthusiasm of "New Labour", appeared unconvinced that taxes were better than regulations. Though its 1990 environment policy statement *An Earthly Chance* accepted the polluter pays principle, it argued that "not all environmental damage can readily be costed in financial terms and billed accordingly. The "polluter pays" principle is a means of attributing responsibility. It leaves open the question of whether it should be implemented through the price mechanism or through regulation". More positively, it stated that "we are attracted to the concept of "green taxes" as a substitute for other forms of taxation so they are fiscally neutral but directed towards environmental objectives". But it specifically ruled out a carbon/energy tax which, it was argued, would drive the UK into recession, reduce competitiveness and fall heavily on the poor.

The think tanks of the Left, however, were attempting to emulate their right-wing counterparts by pressing the case for green taxes. IPPR published a paper in favour of road pricing entitled *A Cleaner, Faster London* in 1989 (Hewitt, 1989) and *Green Taxes: a Budget Memorandum* in 1990 (Owens *et al*, 1990), while the Fabian Society published *Sustainable Development: greening the economy* (Jacobs, 1990) the same year. These challenged the view that regulation was inherently better (from a Left perspective) than taxation. Intervention is needed in the operation of free markets, and the choice of instruments should be made simply on grounds of appropriateness for particular cases.

Rethinking was also underway in environmental groups, particularly Friends of the Earth. *Blueprint* had been greeted with scepticism bordering on hostility, particularly for its argument that a monetary value could be placed on environmental quality. Regulation was seen as a tried-and-tested method, producing secure and predictable outcomes. The argument that taxes were more cost-efficient than regulations cuts little ice with many environmentalists, who see the private sector as rapacious and extremely rich. Nevertheless, it has gradually become more widely recognised that taxes would have to play a role, particularly in persuading consumers to be less profligate. Friends of the Earth's contribution was to confront the issue of equity: would environmental taxes penalise the poor? FoE commissioned the Institute of Fiscal Studies to look into this, resulting in a report called *The Distributional Impact of Environmental Taxes* (Johnson *et al*, 1990) which remains the most influential work in the area. The IFS authors argue that higher petrol prices would be progressive across the population as a whole (though regressive among car drivers), higher food prices would be somewhat regressive, and higher domestic energy prices highly regressive. They also recommended various options for compensation packages.

The various reports and research projects did succeed to an extent in changing the intellectual climate, and blunting some of the previous opposition to green taxation among social policy groups, trade unions and Left politicians. The Labour Party's 1994 environment policy document *In Trust for Tomorrow* was more open to the use of environmental taxes, arguing that they should be used to create markets for certain products, to raise money to fund the clean up of contaminated land and to encourage fuel efficient cars and lower car use.

It is the Liberal Democrats, however, who are the most enthusiastic of the three main parties. This is partly because they have inherited from the Liberal Party a tradition of radical locally-based activist politics which is sympathetic to environmentalism, and partly because they have a commitment to liberal economics which makes them predisposed to favour market mechanisms over regulation. Indeed, an issue combining market economics with environmental concern could have been designed for the Liberal Democrats. It is also fair to say that the Liberal Democrats can afford to be much more open and radical in policy positions than either of the main parties. Their proposals attract much less scrutiny and criticism, because everyone assumes that they will not be implemented – at least not by the Liberal Democrats. The Party is in the unenviable position of a glorified think tank, seeing its ideas adopted by others with never a word of thanks. The fact that the Liberal Democrats have embraced environmental taxation gives some grounds for optimism that a Conservative or Labour government might move in a similar direction at some stage.

Green taxes in the UK

Taxes on resource use are far from new – indeed they predate Pigou's theoretical treatises. Lloyd George's famous People's Budget of 1909, which introduced progressive income tax, also contained the first taxes on petrol. But the explicit linkage between taxes and environmental goals is a more recent phenomenon. And despite the prominence of British economists in developing the intellectual case for environmental taxation, few green taxes have actually been implemented in Britain; we are lagging well behind the more advanced and adventurous countries of Northern Europe. This is partly due to the relative indifference towards environmental issues among British politicians and decision makers – there is a shortage of any instruments of environmental protection, fiscal or regulatory. But it also reflects a predisposition towards regulation, which has a much longer history. The use of coal in London was first restricted in 1228, and the first regulation of sewers was in 1531. Regulation of water pollution was systematised in a series of Acts in 1847–48. The Alkali Act of 1863 required cuts in noxious emissions of 95 per cent.

Nevertheless, there have been some significant environmental tax measures in recent years. Some changes have been introduced under the guise of environmental concern but have in reality been straightforward revenue raisers. With some measures both environmental and revenue-raising motives were present. There is nothing wrong with this; the Government has to get its money from somewhere. Most of those who rail against taxation would not welcome the dismantling of the NHS or the prison service. But there may be tensions between the desire to raise revenue and the desire to improve the environment; a point to which we return below.

Unleaded petrol
The first significant move came in 1987, with the introduction of the tax differential between leaded and unleaded petrol. This was hardly revolutionary in the context of the boldness (or foolhardiness, depending on one's perspective) of other Conservative tax reforms. It was essentially a reactive move; the Government was under pressure from the well-organised and vocal Campaign for Lead Free Air (CLEAR) and felt it had to do something. Nevertheless, it is significant that the response chosen was fiscal rather than regulatory. A tax differential fitted more comfortably into the ideological framework. It was less unacceptable to industry than the alternatives – in particular the mandatory fitting of catalytic converters (which require unleaded petrol), which the British motoring industry was strongly opposing.

The price differential in 1987 was just under 1p a litre; this has increased gradually to just under five pence a litre. It is generally accepted that this first foray into green taxation was a resounding success. The percentage of unleaded petrol increased from less than five per cent to over 50 per cent at the start of 1993 (when the mandatory fitting of catalytic converters to new cars was introduced, making it impossible to attribute further increases in unleaded sales between market and regulatory measures). Lead emissions fell by half. This success is not surprising. For most motorists, substitution was extremely easy, so even a small incentive was enough to change behaviour. It was also a well-publicised change, so that there was a high awareness among drivers that unleaded petrol was now the cheaper option.

The fuel escalator

Despite this early success, and the alleged greening of Margaret Thatcher in the late 1980s, no further green taxes were introduced until 1993. That year, faced with a substantial revenue shortfall, Chancellor Norman Lamont announced in his March Budget that fuel duties would increase in real terms by three per cent in every subsequent budget. No cut-off point was given. His successor Kenneth Clarke increased this "escalator" to five per cent in the November Budget. The fuel escalator is an excellent environmental measure, but it is also an extremely nice earner for the Exchequer: Lamont estimated that his three per cent escalator would net him an extra £1 billion in the third year.

Has the fuel escalator made any difference to fuel use? This is hard to judge, since the things it is trying to affect – fuel efficiency of vehicles and vehicle use – are subject to myriad other factors. Overall petrol consumption fell by four per cent in the first year after the escalator was introduced. But this is unlikely to have been much due to the escalator, which is intended as a long term, gradualist policy. Indeed, the fall had begun in 1991. The escalator has little short term impact on fuel prices, particularly as compared to fluctuations caused by changes in world oil prices.

This is, however, one of its great virtues. Incremental change has proved a relatively painless way of increasing environmental taxation. The escalator has united the political parties (though the Liberal Democrats are concerned about its impact on rural motorists – most of their MPs represent rural constituencies). It provides a good model for how to introduce a new tax. However, it is not clear how widely known it is, and therefore how widely the expectation of higher prices in the future is affecting car model choice or location decisions. Anecdotal evidence suggests that hardly anyone knows about it, and even the car manufacturers, who are obviously aware of it, do not expect a substantial increase in demand for fuel-efficient vehicles and so are not altering their plans. Either the Government needs to do more to publicise the escalator, or it needs to be higher, or both.

VAT on fuel

Lamont also announced that VAT would be extended to domestic energy, first at eight per cent and then at the full rate of 17.5 per cent. He argued that this would help deliver the Government's commitments to reduce CO_2 emissions.

The Labour Party, which had always opposed a carbon tax (the effects of which would have been similar), vigorously attacked the extension of VAT – its task made easier by the fact that the Conservatives had fought and won the recent General Election on a promise not to increase taxes generally and VAT in particular. The impact on the poor was highlighted, and the claim that VAT on fuel was part of the Government's climate change strategy was ridiculed: Robin Cook noted that it had more to do with the public finances going red than Treasury ministers going green. There were indeed considerable grounds for scepticism about the Government's motives. A consultation paper on the climate change strategy, published just three months earlier, had not mentioned extending VAT as a possibility. Even as it introduced the tax, the Government did not claim that it would do much to help the environment, estimating that total carbon emissions would fall by less than one per cent.

The Liberal Democrats also came out against the VAT increase, even though they had supported a carbon/energy tax. Environmental groups were generally agreed that the tax should have been accompanied by regulations and other measures to increase its efficacy, and by a compensation package. But they split in terms of presentation. Friends of the Earth welcomed the tax but called for the accompanying measures to be added. Greenpeace condemned the tax but said it would support it if the other measures were introduced. (This led to a farcical exchange in the House of Commons, with the Prime Minister quoting Friends of the Earth, and the then Leader of the Labour Party, John Smith, quoting Greenpeace back.)

Once it realised the unpopularity of the proposed tax increase, the Government attempted to overcome the problem of regressivity by increasing the budget of the Home Energy Efficiency Scheme, which gives grants to low income households to install insulation and pipe-lagging. The scheme was also extended to include all pensioners, which had political advantages but reduced the funds available to low income households. Energy conservation groups estimated that it would take over a decade to insulate the dwellings of all low-income households – a decade in which the poor would be faced with higher fuel bills.

In the event the Government succeeded in imposing the tax at eight per cent, but was defeated in a vote on its attempt to increase it to 17.5 per cent. It raised virtually no revenue – most had to be conceded to pensioners and the poor in compensation packages. The political price was high: Government popularity plummeted and a series of spectacular by-election losses followed. The environmental price was also high. The scope for sensible debate about environmental taxes has been radically reduced. The impression of a trade-off between environmental protection and social policy, which environmentalists have been striving to overcome for a decade, was reinforced. So too was the widespread view that environmentalism equals sacrifice and so will not be popular with the voters, another misconception which environmentalists have sought mightily to bury.

The landfill tax
The Government's next attempt at environmental taxation was much more successful. From 1996 there will be a tax on landfilled waste of £7 a tonne, with a lower rate of £2 a tonne for inert wastes. About 70 per cent of all controlled waste (ie excluding agricultural waste and mining spoils) is currently sent to landfill; the figure for household waste is 90 per cent. Waste disposal companies will be able to avoid up to 20 per cent of their liability by paying money into special environmental trusts. This is the first new tax introduced specifically for environmental reasons in the UK.

The new landfill tax is a good model of how a tax ought to be introduced. It was announced in 1994, details were announced in 1995 and, following extensive consultation, it is being implemented in 1996. The consultation was genuine, and the design of the tax has been totally altered as a result (it will be based on weight rather than being *ad valorem* as the Government originally proposed). This is a new departure, not only for environmental policy, but for British tax policy generally. Again all political parties have supported it, as have all environmental groups. Even business has not complained too much, although there has been much lobbying on what should constitute inert waste and so be liable for a lower tax rate.

Support for alternative fuels
In his 1995 Budget Kenneth Clarke cut the duty on liquid petroleum gas and natural gas used as transport fuel by 15 per cent.

Green taxes abroad
There are now numerous environmental taxes in use in developed countries (and a smaller number in use in the developing world). The list which follows is far from exhaustive, but gives an idea of the range of economic instruments being used to promote environmental goals. Where available, information on the taxes' environmental impact is also recorded.

Energy and carbon taxes
In 1990 Finland became the first country to introduce a carbon tax – despite the fact that Finland is responsible for only 0.3 per cent of the world's carbon dioxide emissions. The tax rate was originally seven marks (£1.00) per tonne of carbon dioxide; in 1993 the rate was doubled and a new electricity tax of 15 marks (£2.17) per megawatt hour introduced. The energy consumption by industry in relation to value added has been reduced by one third.

A carbon dioxide tax was also introduced in Sweden in 1991, levied as a specific tax on oil, coal, natural gas, bottled gas and petrol. The tax was initially 250 SEK (£24.32) per tonne of CO_2. (This is not a particularly high rate of tax; it is roughly equivalent to 84 US cents per barrel of oil equivalent, so around five per cent given current oil prices of $16 per barrel; the EU's proposed carbon/energy tax would have started at $1 a barrel and increased to $10 per barrel.) Energy-intensive industries were given transitional relief until 1995. Introducing the changes, the Government made clear that it expected the EU to introduce a carbon/energy tax. When it became clear that this was unlikely, Swedish industry was able to pressure the Government to reduce the tax rate paid by industry to 80 SEK. The lost revenue was recouped by raising the rate paid by households (Sterner, 1994). The main impact so far has been on fuel switching, especially in the district heating sector where there has been a switch to biofuels. In 1996 the rate of tax on industry was doubled to 160 SEK (£15.56) per tonne of CO_2.

Norway introduced new energy taxes in 1991. As in Sweden, the package had to be modified after it was introduced, to take account of the impact on energy industries, and to reflect the fact that the EU had not introduced energy taxes as expected.

In 1993 Denmark introduced a CO_2 tax replacing some household energy taxes. The tax was originally 100 DKK (£11.25) per tonne (roughly 40 cents per barrel of oil equivalent or 2.5 per cent); industry paid 50 DKK per tonne and exemptions were available for energy intensive industries. In 1996 the "Danish Energy Package" was implemented; this extended CO_2 and energy taxes to industry and introduced a sulphur tax. The most substantial tax is on energy used by industry for heating purposes; this was taxed at 50 DKK (£5.62) per tonne in 1995, rising to 600 DKK (£67.5) per ton in 2000 – the same rate as households will pay. Light processes will pay 90 DKK (£10.12) per ton for emissions resulting from plant operation, and heavy processes 25 DKK (£2.80) per ton. Companies which agree to make large investments to improve energy efficiency receive a partial rebate. The Government estimates that the new taxes will reduce Danish CO_2 emissions by around five per cent.

In January 1996 the Netherlands introduced a carbon/energy tax on small energy users: households and small commercial establishments. The Government argues that these are sectors which it is difficult to reach with other policy measures such as permits or long-term agreements, but argues also that larger users have been excluded to avoid possible economic damage. The tax is closely modelled on the proposed EU tax, and will eventually reach the same rate of $10 per barrel of oil equivalent. It is levied on final users, but applies only for use between 800–170,000 cubic metres of gas and 800–50,000kWh of electricity. The lower limit is in recognition of the fact that it is not possible to reduce gas or electricity use to zero. From 1997 there will also be a tax on uranium.

Acid rain taxes

A number of countries levy taxes on emissions or sulphur and nitrogen, which cause acid rain. Sweden has a tax on sulphur of SEK 30 (£2.90) per kilo, which has led to a 40 per cent reduction in the sulphur content of fuels, and to an increase in flue-gas cleaning in many plants, and some fuel switching. As a result, the revenue from the tax is considerably less than had been forecast.

Sweden also has a tax on NO_x emissions, levied only on medium and large combustion plants. The aim is to encourage more efficient operation of existing plant and the fitting of new technology. The rate is 40 SEK (£3.62) per tonne of emitted NO_x. The effect has been impressive: even before the tax was introduced in 1992 (but after it had been proposed) measures were taken in the large plants to reduce NO_x emissions, which therefore fell by 35 per cent between 1990 and 1992. "Besides investments in new equipment, the charge has also increased the interest in optimising combustion, in order to minimise NO_x emissions. In some cases the operating staff actually get a bonus on their salary if the NO_x emissions are low. Thus new control systems have been introduced within the firms, as they have economic incentives to keep emissions at the lowest possible level" (Swedish Ministry of the Environment, 1995).

France has charges on both nitrogen and sulphur emissions from large power stations and incinerators, introduced in 1985 and increased in 1990. The rate is now 150 francs (£19) per tonne. Norway and Finland levy sulphur taxes. Poland has a tax of $96 per tonne of sulphur dioxide, which will rise annually 5 per cent above inflation. So far the tax has not been high enough to reduce emissions significantly; it has mainly been a revenue raiser.

Motoring taxes
All countries raise considerable revenue from petrol taxes. Among OECD countries, Portugal has the highest duty, followed by Italy and France. The USA, New Zealand and Japan have the lowest rates. Britain is about average.

Sweden has had a "scrap car charge" since 1975, which aims to prevent cars being dumped. A special charge is levied on sales of new cars, and this is used to finance a premium paid to those who take their cars to authorised scrap yards, provided there are no other unpaid motoring taxes. The charge therefore operates like a deposit scheme. According to the Environment Ministry, the charge has "clearly reduced the number of scrap cars dumped, although there is no reliable information about the actual figure" (Swedish Ministry of the Environment, 1996).

Motorway tolling
Six EU member states, France, Italy, Austria, Spain, Greece and Portugal, use road tolls. This can be a significant revenue raiser: France raises 23 billion francs (£2.92 billion) from motorway tolling.

Urban road pricing
Singapore introduced an Area Licence Scheme in 1975. A fee is payable to enter the city centre from 7.30–10.15 am and 4.30–6.30pm. Between 1974 and 1988 the proportion of journeys into the city centre made by car fell from 43 per cent to 22 per cent, and public transport journeys rose from 46 per cent to 63 per cent. It is planned to transform the scheme into an electronic one.

In a number of Norwegian cities a fee is payable to take a vehicle into the city centre. Payments may be made electronically or at a toll booth. The cost of entering Oslo is roughly £1, with a reduced rate for those with an electronic tag. Austria has announced its intention to introduce electronic road pricing systems before the end of the century.

Air travel taxes

Sweden introduced a tax on emissions from domestic flights in 1989. The tax is levied on emissions of hydrocarbons and nitrogen oxides, and has led to greater attention being paid to pollution reduction by airlines. The tax is under review following Sweden's accession to the EU. Norway has a domestic flight charge (flat rate) on all flights for which rail alternatives exist. A number of German airport authorities have imposed noise charges on landing aircraft. France raises five billion francs from a tax on the use of Paris air space.

Water pollution charges

Germany has an elaborate system of charging for water pollution. Each type of water pollutant in given a weighting, and the charge is then levied per unit. Mercury is 20g per unit, lead is 500g, nitrogen is 25kg. The charge per unit was originally 12 DM (£5.22), and it has increased to 60 DM (£26). A further increase to 70 DM (£30) is scheduled for 1997. Total revenue is 320 million DM (£145 million) a year. France raises 9.4 billion francs (£1.2 billion) a year from water pollution charges.

Product taxes

The Belgian Government passed a law in 1993 allowing the federal government to introduce (with the agreement of the regional governments) a number of product taxes. The taxes are not related in any precise way to the damage caused by products, and are levied only where there are defined alternatives available. So far eco-taxes have been imposed on drinks containers, batteries, throw-away cameras and razors, pesticides and some industrial packaging. A tax on non-recycled paper has been suspended until the end of 1996. The introduction of eco-taxes has been politically fraught, and the products have been chosen on political rather than environmental grounds.

All the Scandinavian countries have taxes on drinks sold in disposable containers. Sweden has a charge on environmentally harmful batteries. The tax has led to substitution of less harmful nickel-hybrid batteries for mercury and nickel-cadmium batteries. Italy has a tax of 100 Lire (around four pence, or five times the manufacturing cost) on non-biodegradable plastic bags.

Agricultural input taxes

Austria introduced a small fertiliser levy in 1986. Despite the low level of the tax, it has had a significant effect on fertiliser use. Sweden has had fertiliser taxes since 1982, to combat eutrophication of inland waterways and the Baltic and North Seas. The purpose was partly to reduce use and partly to finance clean-up operations. At their peak (in 1991) the taxes were between 30–35 per cent of the sales value, but the level has now fallen to 10–13 per cent. There has been a significant fall in fertiliser use – 25 per cent for nitrogen, 65 per cent for phosphorus, 60 per cent for potassium. (Some of this is accounted for by a reduction in land under cultivation.) Norway and Finland also have fertiliser taxes, while Denmark has a pesticides tax.

Waste taxes

Denmark has waste disposal taxes on both landfill and incineration. The taxes were introduced in 1986 at a low rate (40 DKK (£4.50)/tonne), and have risen substantially since, to 195 DKK (£21.90) for landfill and 160 DKK (£18) for incineration. In 1997 they will rise again, to 295 DKK (£33) for landfill, 210 DKK (£24) for incineration and 160 DKK (£18) for incineration with energy recovery. (The disposal fee for landfill, pre-tax, is 150-250 DKK (£17–28) per tonne; for incineration 150–300 DKK (£17–34) per tonne.) The tax levels are much higher than the UK rate of £7 per tonne, even though pre-tax landfill prices are broadly similar. In the commercial and industrial sector, where waste producers bear the increased charges directly, the impact has been dramatic. Twenty-six per cent of commercial and industrial waste was recycled in 1985; in 1993 this had increased to 61 per cent. Recycling of demolition waste increased from 12 per cent to 82 per cent. Households are not charged by volume, so there has been relatively little impact in this sector.

The Netherlands has a landfill tax of 29.20 DFL (£11.60) per tonne. France has a waste storage tax and an industrial waste tax of 40 Francs (£5).

Local and regional green taxes

A number of countries regard environmental taxes as appropriate to be given wholly or partly to sub-central government. There are constraints, of course: different environmental tax regimes can distort patterns of economic activity between localities, and different excise duties can lead to a localised version of cross-border shopping. Against this, local authority powers in this area allow for experimentation and innovation through diversity in a way which is impossible in an over-centralised state such as the UK. The following list gives an idea of environmental taxes which are operated at a sub-central level.

The German *Land* of Baden-Wurtemberg introduced a tax on hazardous waste in 1991. In 1993 the rates were increased; they now stand at 100 DM (£43.50), 200 DM (£87) or 300 DM (£130.50) per tonne, depending on the hazardousness of the waste. In 1992 waste fell from 605,000 tonnes to 430,000, and in 1993 to 354,000 tonnes. Revenues were 32.2 DM million (£14 million) in 1993 and 36.7 DM million (£15.96) in 1994 (due to the rise in rates).

The German City of Kassell introduced a tax on disposable plates, cutlery and take-away food and drinks in 1992.

French *departements* can levy a tax on construction on greenfield sites; communes can levy an "over-construction" tax on developers; both communes and departements can levy a tourist tax (maximum of seven francs per night), a tax on skiing equipment and a tax on physical advertising.

Irish counties have been active in using green taxes to finance water treatment and waste management operations. Their activism has been driven in part by the fact that their main source of revenue, domestic rates, has been abolished and replaced by block grants from the centre, which have not been maintained in real terms. Three Irish counties: Waterford, Wexford and Monaghan, have introduced schemes under which households are charged for waste collection on a per-bag or per-bin basis. Contrary to expectations, this has not led to an increase in fly-tipping – indeed people have been more willing to inform the authorities about fly-tippers, because they are unwilling to pay the tax themselves and see others evade it. There has also been little public resistance to the notion of paying by volume for waste disposal (Convery and Rooney, 1996).

The Catalan government initiated a volume-based waste water charging system for households and industry in 1983. Households pay a fixed rate per cubic metre, businesses a rate based on volume and degree of contamination. Galicia has experimented with sulphur taxes. The Canadian province of Saskatchewan has a deposit refund scheme and a tax on disposable packaging. In Greece, Athens and Evora have introduced special water pricing regimes to conserve water in times of drought.

Perverse exemptions and subsidies

Despite the growing recognition that tax systems have a pervasive influence on the quality of the environment, there are still numerous specific taxes or subsidies which have undesirable effects on behaviour. The most visible of these are in the transport sector: a number of countries give preferential tax treatment to company cars, which encourage people to drive larger models, and to drive further than necessary, both of which result in higher levels of pollution. In Britain, for example, there is an incentive to drive further than 18,000 miles in a company car. In addition, six EU member states recognise the cost of commuting to and from work as a professional expense which can be deducted from an employee's taxable income. This in effect gives a subsidy to those living a long distance from their work place, and contributes to an inefficient use of the transport system. In Germany, the use of a car is rewarded with a tax deduction that is five times higher than that for a bicycle – although some of this advantage, especially for larger cars, was eroded by the 1996 Budget.

The IMF has called on governments to reduce these subsidies as a means of greening the tax system and extending the tax base (IMF, 1994). Tax subsidies for commuting by car were reduced in Sweden as part of the package of new environmental taxes.

There are also subsidies for the energy industry in most producer countries. The European Commission calculated that in 1992 coal production was subsidies by £16 a tonne in France, £21 a tonne in Spain and £51 a tonne in Germany (Parker, 1994).

Many environmental taxes exempt key polluting sectors. Catalonia's waste water charges do not apply to agriculture. Portugal's taxation of high-sulphur fuel oil exempts the power generation sector, the largest user. Belgium has a pesticides tax which exempts farmers!

All fiscal systems also have oddities, inconsistencies and distortions which encourage perverse or undesirable behaviour, even though this is not the intention of the public authorities. These are the tax cock-ups rather than the tax conspiracies. In the UK VAT is payable at the full rate on energy savings material such as insulation, but at a reduced rate on fuel. Those refurbishing properties pay VAT at the full rate; those building new properties pay no VAT at all.

The carbon/energy tax proposal

Recent debate about extending environmental taxation has been dominated by the European Commission's carbon/energy tax proposal. In 1991 the Commission proposed a new tax to be introduced in stages, starting at $3 per barrel of oil equivalent in 1993, and rising $1 a year until it reached $10 per barrel in 2000. The tax was to reflect both carbon and energy content of fuel. Nuclear power would have paid only the energy part; renewables were exempted. Revenues would have accrued to member states, and the Commission stressed that these should be used to reduce other taxes, not increase expenditure.

Discussion has been going on, at varying levels of intensity, ever since. The UK led the opposition, on the grounds that "Brussels" should not be involved in tax matters, but other states, notably Spain, were concerned about some of the proposal's economic implications. In 1994 the draft Directive was withdrawn, but discussions on alternative ways forward continued. The European Council agreed a statement at Essen in December 1994:

> The European Council has taken note of the Commission's intention of submitting guidelines to enable every member state to apply a CO_2/energy tax on the basis of common parameters if it so desires...In order to achieve the Community [CO_2] stabilisation target, the Council deems taxation measures necessary. In this respect, a Community framework should be developed.

The statement goes on to consider how such tax measures should be introduced. It is clear from this that while the proposal for a binding EU-wide carbon/energy tax may be dormant, the pressure within Europe for measures on energy taxation will continue.

The Belgian and Dutch ministers of finance have suggested a framework agreement which would allow co-ordinated but optional action. The

German government has been pressing for an agreement to raise the minimum tax rates on mineral oil, and an extension of this tax to gas and coal. The lowest rate of tax in a member state is 20 per cent higher than the minimum currently stipulated, so the agreement is meaningless except as a theoretical floor. The UK government opposed this proposal; so too did Spain and Portugal, ostensibly on grounds of sovereignty, but probably also because they are concerned about the impact of energy taxes on their economic development.

In May 1995 the Commission presented a revised proposal, in which it proposed that "the implementation of a harmonised tax be preceded by a transitional period" – with the tax being harmonised in 2000. Spain, which was then President of the Council and which had previously been sceptical of the tax, supported the new proposal, as did Germany, Sweden, Denmark, Finland, Belgium, the Netherlands and Austria. The UK and France remained opposed.

In March 1996 the Council of Economic and Finance ministers asked the Commission to come forward with new proposals before the end of the year. However, Single Market Commissioner Mario Monti subsequently suggested that this might have been because they were unable to agree on anything more specific – which does not bode well for agreement on any revised version which the Commission submits, since any agreement would have to be reached on the basis of unanimity. So progress is more likely at national level.

Why aren't green taxes more common?

Despite the examples of green taxes listed earlier, environmental taxes are much less widespread than their theoretical attractions would lead one to expect. There is a noticeable reluctance among politicians to implement new measures. In the 1990 White Paper *This Common Inheritance*, for example, most discussion of environmental taxation was contained in an appendix. Despite numerous promises to consider this, explore that and consult on the other, there were no commitments to action.

This is not due solely to politicians' lack of interest in environmental matters, though this has undoubtedly played a part. Even in environmentally-conscious states like Germany, there have been relatively few green taxes. As Stephen Smith comments in a study of Germany: "Despite [the] substantial catalogue of comprehensive proposals, and the vigorous debate during the late 1980s, only a limited number of environmental tax measures have in practice been introduced" (Smith, 1995). What, then, are the problems with environmental taxes? The next chapter will examine some of the arguments commonly used against them.

3. Arguments against environmental taxation

This chapter examines some of the most common arguments against environmental taxation. Some environmentalists argue that taxes are a less effective way of securing environmental goals than regulations, and that taxation requires a monetary valuation to be placed on priceless natural assets. Many businesses argue that environmental taxes would be bad for competitiveness. And there is a widespread perception that environmental taxation is inherently regressive.

Regulation is a better way to protect the environment

There has been a long-running academic debate between the relative merits of regulation and taxation as a means of combating environmental problems. As noted above, proponents of taxation argue that a tax will reduce pollution at least cost to society. Proponents of regulation argue that it offers greater certainty, and that if something is damaging, it ought simply to be banned.

This debate misses the essential point. Faced with an environmental problem, governments have a choice of four strategies: do nothing (the one normally adopted); introduce a regulation; introduce a market mechanism; introduce a package of measures including both regulations and market mechanisms. The most appropriate strategy will depend on this case in question. As the Treasury puts it: "In practice regulation or economic instruments such as tradeable permits or subsidies will sometimes be the most efficient way of achieving environmental objectives. The best combination of economic instruments and regulation will vary from case to case" (Treasury, 1996).

In many cases, and certainly the main issues such as energy conservation, managing demand for transport or minimising waste, a combination of market mechanisms and regulation will be the most efficient and effective way to meet environmental objectives. The reason many regulations have failed, or succeeded only partially, is because they are going against the grain of existing price signals. For example, the Corporate Average Fuel Efficiency (CAFE) standards in the USA have made little progress in raising fuel efficiency of vehicles because low gasoline prices mean that there is very little consumer demand for more miles-per-gallon. Getting the environmental prices right is therefore an essential part of making existing environmental protection regimes work more effectively. But environmental taxes will almost always be more effective and more efficient in meeting environmental goals if they are backed up by a strong and sensible regulatory regime.

A good example of this is pollution from road transport. The mandatory fitting of catalytic converters to all new cars was a significant step forward in cutting pollution, and there are other regulatory measures which should be taken. The practice of adding carcinogenic benzene to petrol in order to boost vehicle performance should be banned forthwith – it is one of the starkest examples of private sector irresponsibility to have emerged in recent years. Minimum standards for fuel efficiency should be introduced. Traffic management measures should be used vigorously and imaginatively. But even if all this is done, there will still be scope for taxation to reduce pollution further – by encouraging motorists to choose less polluting vehicles and to use their cars more sparingly, or even to drive them more slowly.

An illustration of the need to mix taxes and regulations is given in economic modelling of the Polish town of Krakow's policies for combating sulphur dioxide pollution, carried out by London Economics. According to the study, meeting air quality standards through command and control policies would cost £28 million per year, and through a fuel tax on all sources £24 million per year. However, the fuel tax would have to be around £1,000 per tonne of sulphur dioxide to achieve this, and would lead to results which would not be economically efficient or socially just. Imposing a ban on coal burning in households or other sources in the city centre (as was done in the 1956 Clean Air Act in London) would mean that the tax had to be only £270 per tonne to meet the target. A mixed approach, with regulation for small sources and taxation for larger ones, reduces the overall cost of compliance to £22 million a year, 21 per cent lower than regulation alone and seven per cent lower than taxation alone (Pototschnig, 1996).

It is true that regulation delivers greater certainty of outcome than taxation, provided that the regulations are properly enforced (though taxes also have to be enforced, a point which often appears to elude their more enthusiastic proponents). But not all environmental policies require the same degree of certainty. In the late 1980s it was decided that the use of CFCs needed to be reduced very quickly, and phased out over a decade. Most countries therefore introduced regulations to ensure that this occurred. If a substance or activity needs to be reduced to zero, it is simpler and cheaper to ban it than to tax it. But where the need is to reduce rather than eliminate something, the economic advantages of taxation come into play. Energy use and transport both come into this category.

If a government has a specific level to which it has to reduce pollution, and a lower level to which it would like to reduce it, it can use regulation to secure the essential reduction and taxation to secure the desirable reduction. Tradeable permits combine the flexibility of taxes with the certainty of outcome of regulation, and are another option to be considered. But in many cases the location of pollution matters as well as the total amount (this is true of both sulphur dioxide and NO_x, for example), so restrictions would have to be imposed on trading, leading to greater administrative complexity. In cases where the location is irrelevant – CO_2, for example – there may be so many polluters than simple tax would be more efficient. However, tradeable permits might be appropriate for securing CO_2 reductions from the heaviest users.

Green taxes would have to be extremely high

Some critics of environmental taxation have argued that taxes would have little impact on behaviour unless they were set at unrealistically high levels. A number of studies lend credence to this argument: one 1989 study predicted that a tax of $623 (£402) per ton of carbon would lead to a reduction of only 26 per cent in emissions (Howarth *et al*, 1989).

The behavioural response depends on the nature of the activity or product being taxed (how essential is it?), the availability and cost of alternatives, public/corporate awareness of the issue and the tax, and many other factors. The small price differential in favour of unleaded petrol was sufficient to boost demand substantially, but this is not surprising, since there were few obstacles to changing behaviour.

In some cases a tax will have little impact on behaviour because the structure of the market means that producers absorb it and do not pass it on to consumers; it then becomes in effect a tax on profits. This is not in itself an argument against the tax, but it is an argument against using it to secure environmental goals.

In other cases taxes may have little impact because the value of a product or activity to the consumer is such that it is worth paying the tax. In these cases a Government can impose a tax in order to make the polluter pay, perhaps to fund remediation work or compensate those damaged by the pollution. If the public interest requires that the pollution is reduced or ended, the product or activity will need to be regulated or banned.

However, in general the argument that environmental taxes will have little impact on behaviour depends on the assumption that the tax will be introduced in isolation, with no accompanying measures to increase the impact. In practice this is unlikely, and it certainly is not recommended. Regulations should be used to increase the efficacy of environmental taxes by increasing the elasticity of demand for the activity being taxed. An energy tax will be more effective when backed by minimum efficiency standards for buildings and appliances. Higher petrol prices will be more effective when combined with sensible land use planning policies. Waste taxes will work better if there are also rules on the recycled content of certain products. And so on.

Governments should also undertake public information and education campaigns to back-up the price signal. There have been a number of government campaigns encouraging people to save energy. But more information is essential if individuals are to make informed and responsible choices; schemes like the EU's eco-labels and energy labels are important in this regard.

The behavioural impact of environmental taxes will also be increased the longer they are in force. It is clear that there are infrastructural and capital constraints which make it difficult for individuals and companies to react to rapid changes. If a company has invested in an energy-intensive production process, it will not be in a position to change to a different process just because the price of energy goes up. Demand is particularly inelastic if there is an expectation that a price increase will be reversed fairly quickly.

The picture is very different if higher prices persist, and if there is widespread expectation that they will persist. Then it will become worth a company's while investing in energy efficiency equipment. As the investment cycle passes, the company will acquire more efficient machinery. So taxes are only likely to benefit the environment if they are introduced on a long-term basis, with a degree of political consensus such that individuals and firms do not expect them to be reversed. Since the expectation of future price levels is almost as important as the fact of existing price levels, environmental taxes can sensibly be phased in gradually, to minimise transitional costs and allow people time to adapt.

The substantial increase in the price of oil which occurred in 1973 meant that many countries implemented energy efficiency programmes for the rest of that decade. Between 1973 and 1983, total primary energy consumption declined in the United States and Germany by five per cent, in the United Kingdom by 14 per cent and in Sweden by 19 per cent. And there is a clear correlation between the price of energy and the use of energy. Countries with higher energy prices, like Japan, Italy and Germany use less energy per unit of GDP than countries with low energy prices like the USA or Australia (Hoeller and Coppel, 1992). Over the medium term, demand for energy is not as inelastic as is often claimed.

Much the same can be said of demand for petrol. Short term price increases will have little effect – individuals have invested in a particular vehicle which cannot suddenly be made more efficient (although it can be driven more slowly). They also have set patterns of commuting and so on which cannot easily be altered. If the higher price persists, however, there will be consumer demand for more efficient models, and transport patterns will change. One study calculates that a ten per cent increase in fuel prices leads, over time, to a seven per cent decrease in fuel used. (Goodwin, 1992) Another study, of 14 different countries, found a strong negative correlation between fuel price and fuel use per head. (Von Weizacker and Jesinghaus, 1992). The Royal Commission Report on Transport and the Environment predicts the reductions in petrol use arising from the fuel escalator to be four per cent by 2000 and 21 per cent by 2020.

The same picture emerges if one considers the likely impact of waste taxes. The impact of a landfill tax on demand for landfill space was estimated by consultants Coopers and Lybrand in a report for the Department of the Environment. They conclude that demand will be unresponsive in the short term, and will remain unresponsive in low-cost rural areas, but will become much more responsive in high-cost urban areas in the longer term, particularly if public policy is used to develop better recycling facilities. (Coopers and Lybrand, 1993). Again this demonstrates the need for environmental taxes to be in effect for the long term, and to be introduced in conjunction with other, non-fiscal policy measures.

Should a monetary value be placed on the environment?

The notion of internalising external costs which is at the core of the economist's case for environmental taxation has led to some complex, even tortuous, attempts to place a monetary value on the true costs of some activities, involving calculations about what people say they would be willing to pay to see things preserved (which depends, of course, on how rich they are, and thus gives the wishes of the rich greater value than those of the poor) or how much they would be willing to accept in compensation (which gives everyone a *de facto* veto). Such valuation techniques cannot take account of the wishes of future generations, nor do they generally bother to take account of the wishes of peasants living in far-off countries like Bangladesh, who would presumably want a great deal of compensation for the fact that their home may be inundated by rising sea levels.

Placing a monetary value on, say, Twyford Down, the survival of a species or a human life is inevitably controversial and subjective, and many environmentalists reject the entire concept of cost-benefit analysis. The Department of Transport in particular is guilty of presenting a series of often spurious calculations about the costs and benefits of a new road as incontrovertible fact. The inclusion in the 1995 Environment Act of a requirement for the new Environment Agency to take account of the costs of its proposed actions – on the face of it a fairly commonsense proposition – caused outrage among environmental lobbyists.

Outright rejection of the concept of valuing the environment would be going too far. The problem at present is precisely that the environment, having no calculated value, is assumed to be worth nothing. But it should be recognised that measuring environmental costs and benefits is a question of broad estimate rather than exact calculation. Policy makers should avoid being drawn into arcane disputes about the exact level of externalities associated with particular activities; this can be used as a way of avoiding having to take any action. Even if an exact figure could be agreed (which it cannot), it is unlikely that a tax of this level would be introduced, since taxation needs to reflect wider social, industrial and fiscal considerations. The important point is for governments to recognise the need to provide an incentive for polluters to consider the impact of their actions, not to strike theological poses about the precise external costs of pollution.

Behind the objection to techniques of monetary valuation is an assumption that those who want to use environmental taxation for some things want to use it for everything. Some things are indeed too precious to be counted in monetary terms. There is no tax which would be high enough to capture the external costs of building a motorway up Ben Nevis – or, indeed, a railway up Cairn Gorm. But to argue from this that a tax which increases the price of petrol in order to improve urban air quality is in some sense sacrilegious, disrespectful of nature, is far-fetched. Not every facet of the natural environment is priceless; trade-offs do have to be made.

Environmental taxes damage competitiveness

This is not, generally, an argument against environmental taxation *per se*, but against any measures to protect the environment. Those lobbying hard against particular environmental taxes are often those who, in other contexts, wax lyrical about the superiority of market mechanisms over "command and control" regulations.

To the extent that generalisations can be made, it is fair to say that British industry has adopted a negative attitude towards environmental policies. Despite mounting evidence that, in the CBI's phrase, *Environment means Business*, that there is money to be saved or made in taking the environment seriously, British industry has generally regarded proposals for new environmental policies with hostility, seeing them as inevitably leading to higher costs and reduced competitiveness. Companies and their associations have accepted the general case that market mechanisms are more efficient than regulations, but proceeded to argue against every particular market mechanism that is proposed. (A good example is a paper from the Economics Unit of BP (1995) which argues convincingly the need for environmental taxation, but proceeds to reject the proposed European carbon/energy tax.)

There is a great deal of misrepresentation and special pleading on this subject, and the impact of environmental costs on competitiveness is often exaggerated. The changes in industrial costs arising from environmental taxes will be, for most sectors, a very small percentage of overall costs. Exchange rate fluctuations are likely to have a far more substantial impact on competitiveness than marginal changes in tax rates. An OECD report on *Environmental Policies and Industrial Competitiveness* concludes that there has been "little or no impact on the overall competitiveness of countries" (OECD, 1993a).

There is an argument that UK firms might currently be struggling to compete, that any increase in costs will be damaging – the straw that breaks the camel's back. It is not clear why this should be so, however. British industry has a lighter tax burden than industry in most of our main competitors – 5.9 per cent of GDP compared to 7.2 per cent in the US, 9.1 per cent in Germany, 9.4 per cent in Japan, 14.5 per cent in France (defined as the sum of corporation tax, payroll taxes and employers' social security contributions).

Moreover, higher standards could actually be beneficial for the competitiveness of British business. As the OECD report points out:

In general, pollution and resource degradation represent a form of economic waste and inefficient use of resources; environmental measures can spur firms to develop more resource-efficient methods of production and reduce costs... In Japan, for example, pressure to increase energy efficiency and lower pollution has reduced energy and raw material inputs to Japanese-produced goods and yielded competitive cost advantages.

(OECD, 1993a)

It is likely that sudden changes in the cost of energy in one country but not in others will have an impact on that country's ability to compete. The impact of gradual increases, leaving industry time to adapt, is less clear. Those countries with high energy prices, such as Germany and Japan, are more competitive and wealthier than low-cost nations, as the graph below shows. While this correlation is not conclusive and does not imply simple causation, it suggests at the very least that there is no necessary link between low energy prices and economic success.

Nevertheless, the impact on industrial costs will need to be taken into account, not least for political reasons. No politician is likely, in the current climate, to support environmental taxation which leads to a significant

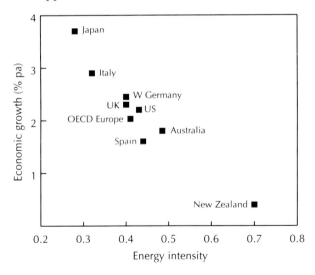

Fig 3.1 Energy intensity and economic growth
Source: IEA, Paris and Barker, 1992

increase in the fiscal burden on industry. Does this mean that green taxes for the corporate sector have to be ruled out, or postponed until agreement on co-ordinated action is reached with key competitors? Such agreement is likely to be hard to achieve.

Fortunately there is a way around the difficulty. Some environmental taxes are needed to raise extra revenue for specific environment-related purposes – road pricing to fund public transport subsidies, for example. But in general it is possible to envisage a shift in the burden of taxation, so that some taxes are reduced as others are increased. If other corporate taxes – Employers' National Insurance, Corporation Tax or Business Rates – were reduced as environmental taxes were phased in, the overall impact on business would be neutral. Thus the question of whether environmental taxes hurt competitiveness cannot be divorced from the question of what is done with the revenues. This is the issue to which we return in the next chapter.

The sectoral impact
Even if one accepts that the overall impact on competitiveness could be neutral, it is clear that some industries will be seriously affected: sectors which are energy intensive and highly traded such as chemicals, non-ferrous metals, mining, pulp and paper. Sectors which are already labour-intensive, such as telecommunications, retailing, tourism and many public services, will gain (OECD, 1993a).

There are a number of ways in which the specific problems with competitiveness for these sectors could be overcome. One option would be to impose border tax adjustments, to ensure that imported goods paid a similar tax on energy content. This is no longer an option within the EU, which suggests that this type of tax should ideally be set in Brussels. Countervailing duties might also fall foul of GATT rules – although they might not: it all depends on the interpretation of certain key clauses, and on whether energy used is regarded as part of the product or part of the process. One of the problems with GATT is that its rules are so complex and opaque, as the following paragraph will demonstrate.

In the past GATT has allowed a US import charge on chemical derivatives on the grounds that it was equal to a "like" charge imposed on chemicals sold within the US. This suggests that a border tax adjustment imposed, for example, by the EU to match an EU energy tax would not be discriminatory. But things are not, sadly, so simple. If the EU imposed a tax on imports from a state which already taxed energy in a similar manner (Japan, say), then "A clear case for discrimination under [GATT] could be made, on the basis that the imported product is being taxed twice while the domestic product is being taxed only once" (Cameron, Demaret and Geradin, 1994). Moreover, another ruling (the "tuna/dolphin case") ruled that it is a breach of GATT rules to discriminate between like products on the basis of their methods of production. "The broad implications of this ruling are that GATT contracting parties cannot discriminate between physically identical products, which differ in terms of the environmental impacts caused during their production and processing" (Arden Clark, 1994). Since energy use appears to be part of the process, this appears to rule out border tax adjustments to reflect an energy tax. However, a footnote to Annexe II of the Uruguay Round Agreement on Subsidies and Countervailing Measures states that inputs such as energy, fuels and oils, although not physically incorporated in the final product, are consumed in the same way as inputs which are incorporated in the final product. This appears to re-open the door to border tax adjustments to reflect an energy tax.

Not surprisingly, the debate about trade and environmental protection is continuing, particularly in the context of international environmental treaties such as the Montreal Protocol. The OECD has recognised that in some cases trade measures relating to production processes, rather than final products, should be allowed in international environmental agreements (OECD, 1995). It is almost inevitable that any measure taken by the EU would be challenged under GATT, so that there would eventually have to be a ruling by the World Trade Organisation. It is impossible to say what this ruling would be, but the likelihood of a legal challenge is no reason not to proceed, though Britain alone could not impose countervailing duties on imports from other EU states.

An alternative approach, included in the European Commission carbon/energy tax proposal, is to make any new tax conditional on similar measures being adopted in the main competitor economies. This would certainly remove concerns about competitive impact, but would make progress extremely difficult to achieve. Agreement even among European governments has so far proved elusive, and imposing a requirement to co-ordinate action with the United States (particularly with the anti-environmental feeling in Congress) and others would effectively be a recipe for inaction. There may be more sense in a British government introducing such a "conditionality clause" regarding other EU states, but this would rightly be seen as procrastination unless it was coupled with support for an EU energy tax and the introduction of majority voting for environmental taxation.

A third alternative – again included in the Commission proposal – would be to grant exemptions to energy-intensive or other particularly effected sectors. This is broadly the way in which Scandinavia and the Netherlands have dealt with this problem. However, it would rather destroy the environmental impact of the tax measure, leaving the heaviest polluters without any incentive to reduce energy use. It would also give rise to new political difficulties, since there would be ferocious lobbying by some sectors wishing to gain exclusion.

If any exemptions are granted, they should be temporary, designed to give energy intensive industries time to adjust (although the phasing in of new taxes would give them time anyway). A better approach, if exemptions are thought to be absolutely necessary, would be to exempt only a set amount of energy (per unit of production). This would mean that companies still had an incentive to reduce energy use above this. Energy intensive processes such as cement manufacture, steel or chemicals can be made much more energy efficienct. Such processes could also be given the option of installing their own energy generators – if these were renewable sources, they could be exempted from the tax.

Environmental taxes are regressive

The final and, in the UK context, most widely heard argument against environmental taxes is that they hurt the poor. Public support for the concept of "fair taxation" remains strong, as the Conservatives discovered when they introduced a poll tax – an approach which had offended medieval conceptions of social justice, and was therefore unlikely to appeal in the marginally more enlightened 20th Century. Conceptions of fairness were also instrumental in defeating the Government's attempt to implement the second tranche of VAT on domestic fuel. The concept of progressive taxation is supported by substantial majorities in all EU countries – 87 per cent in Germany, 85 per cent in the UK, 84 per cent in Italy (Lansley and Gowan, 1994).

An exception to this general support for progressive taxation appears to be made for "sin taxes" on tobacco and alcohol. Public acceptance of these is so strong that it overrides concerns about distributive justice which in other contexts are regarded as paramount. When the Government was defeated on the second tranche of VAT on domestic fuel, the Chancellor introduced instead a package including higher taxes on alcohol and tobacco which were more regressive in their impact than the original measure. But because fuel is essential, whereas tobacco and alcohol are thought not to be, there was little protest.

The UK tax system has become more regressive in recent years. In 1979, the top fifth of the population (in terms of income) paid 38 per cent of their income in tax, while the bottom fifth paid only 31 per cent. By 1992, the figure was 34 per cent for the top fifth and 39 per cent for the bottom fifth. Broadly regressive changes have included a steady shift from direct to indirect taxes, reductions in top rates of income tax and the freezing of the lower rate threshold in 1993 and 1994.

There are, however, different ways of looking at progressivity and regressivity. One way, the theoretical approach, is to look simply at the incidence of taxation. An income tax is more progressive than a sales tax. A second, more practical way is to look at what the government proposes to do with the revenues. A package in which the government levies income tax and uses the revenue to subsidise opera tickets is less progressive than a package in which the government levies a sales tax and uses the revenue to pay welfare benefits to the poor.

Of course, the most progressive package would be one in which the government levied an income tax and used it to pay welfare benefits. This has been the traditional approach of the left, the heart of social democracy. It should certainly not be abandoned. Indeed, at a time of widening inequality there is a need for more rather than less redistribution of income and wealth. However, the political constraints need to be recognised. Not all the expenditure a progressive government would like to take can be funded through direct taxation. In this situation, one has to weigh up the social cost of inaction as well as the impact of a tax increase. For example, the lack of books in state schools is highly regressive in its impact – richer parents buy their children either the books or a place in a private school. Unreliable and expensive public transport is primarily of concern to the one-third of households who do not own cars, which are predominantly (though not exclusively) those in lower income groups. Would it be progressive or regressive to impose an indirect tax in order to increase spending on education or public transport? This is a question which cannot be answered in the abstract. (See Corry D (1995): *Indirect taxes are not as bad as you think*, printed as an appendix to this report.)

Environmental taxes have been criticised by some on the Left as "rationing by price". This is a strange statement. In a market economy, that is how most goods and services are apportioned. There are some things, like health and education, which should be outside the market – free at the point of use. But none of the candidates for environmental taxation comes into this category. Road use is currently free, but food is "rationed by price". Which is the more essential? Genuine rationing – rationing by coupon – would be more equitable. It would also be politically impossible, and in any case not ideal. If the coupons were tradeable, the rich would end up with them anyway, though the poor would have more money from the sale of their coupons. A non-tradeable system would simply drive trading underground.

As argued in Chapter One, current environmental patterns are highly inequitable, with poor households suffering more from pollution, local environmental degradation, and so on. One has to ask, therefore, whether environmental taxation is more regressive than inaction. The answer, of course, is that sometimes it is, sometimes it is not. It all depends on the nature of the problem and the nature of the tax.

One also has to consider whether environmental taxation is more regressive than the equivalent environmental regulation. Again this is impossible to answer in the abstract, so we will consider the case of transport. Let us assume that we want to tackle pollution and urban congestion. The options available are taxes or road pricing, minimum fuel efficiency standards, mandatory pollution controls on vehicles, and traffic bans. The impact of transport taxation on low income households in considered in detail below; for now it is sufficient to note that higher taxes will be progressive across the population as a whole (since the poor cannot afford cars) but regressive among car drivers. Banning cars in urban areas would in a sense be more equitable – though if taxis were allowed it could be said to discriminate against those unable to afford taxi fares. Efficiency standards and pollution controls could also be said to be even-handed in their impact (although if as the car manufacturers claim they will make vehicles more expensive there will be a regressive impact at the point of purchase). So should one reject taxation and opt instead for these regulations? The answer is that one should not – one should go for both taxation and regulation, because they are not really equivalent at all. Traffic-free city centres are greatly to be desired, but much of the traffic will then be displaced into the suburbs. Greater fuel efficiency and stricter emissions standards are similarly to be welcomed, but without policies which manage demand for transport their impact will be overwhelmed by increases in vehicle numbers – as is predicted to happen with catalytic converters. To say that environmental regulation is less regressive than taxation is like saying that the Government health warning on cigarette packets is less regressive than tobacco taxes: it may be true, but it is not very relevant, since the one will not be effective without the other.

The blanket assertion that environmental taxation is regressive, therefore, oversimplifies the picture. Cuts in government expenditure or a failure to act to protect the environment may be even more regressive. The distributional impact of green taxes should be assessed on a case-by-case basis.

Some environmental taxes will fall on business – taxes on toxic emissions, for example – so the regressive impact will be limited. An increase in business costs is likely to be mildly regressive if it feeds through into higher prices to the consumer, but a tax reform which redistributes rather than increases business taxes will have a broadly neutral impact on prices.

Other environmental taxes will fall indirectly on individuals, but can be collected through a progressive mechanism. An example is a landfill tax, which will increase the cost to local authorities of disposing of municipal waste (although most of the impact will be on the industrial sector). The local authority will be able to recoup its costs through local taxation, be it property or income based. Unfortunately, in the UK local taxation is itself not very progressive, but this need not be the case. Alternatively, if the tax is levied centrally, central government could choose to use some of the revenue to increase its support revenues to local authorities. Nevertheless, there are legitimate concerns about the impact of some green taxes.

Domestic energy taxes

The main areas of concern are the taxation of domestic energy, and transport taxes. Environmentalists and opposition politicians may have argued, correctly, that the British Government's decision to impose VAT on domestic fuel was motivated by financial rather than environmental considerations. But the fact remains that other proposals for energy taxation, such as the European Commission's carbon/energy tax proposal would have had a broadly similar impact on domestic energy prices (albeit phased in over a longer period).

The Government argued that most other European countries have a tax on domestic fuel. But it ignored a crucial difference. Other Northern European countries with climates similar to or colder than Britain's have far stricter regulations governing the insulation standards of their housing stock. They simply do not have the draughty, damp and impossible-to-heat properties which are so common in the UK. Energy use is therefore much more closely correlated to income – those who use more energy do so because they own more appliances or indulge in more luxuries. Until Britain reaches similar levels of energy efficiency with our housing stock, comparisons with domestic energy taxation in other Northern European countries will be fairly bogus.

The social impact of higher fuel bills in the UK is illustrated by a study carried out at the University of York's Social Policy Research Unit (Hutton and Hardman, 1993). The survey found that those households with incomes in the top 20 per cent spend 4.2 per cent of their budget on fuel, while those in the lowest 20 per cent spend 12.1 per cent. The burden is therefore nearly three times greater for low income households than for more affluent households. Only 46 per cent of those in the lowest quintile have gas central heating (the most energy efficient form of space heating); the figure for the highest quintile is 75 per cent.

There are also different impacts for different types of household. Families with children spend over £13 a week on fuel, while pensioners and single householders spend £8–£10 a week. Single pensioners spend 16 per cent of their budget on fuel, as do lone parents with children under five. Those living in private rented accommodation – the most energy inefficient form of tenure – also have proportionately high fuel bills, and less incentive to invest in efficiency measures, since they may not stay in the property long enough to reap the benefits. These figures illustrate the difficulty of designing a targeted compensation package.

Low income households are less able to cut back on fuel use by changing equipment or installing energy efficiency measures, which can have a high capital cost. Indeed, energy use in the domestic sector overall is far less responsive to price than energy use in the industrial and commercial sectors (DTI, 1995).

An eco-bonus

The low elasticity, together with the regressive impact of higher domestic fuel costs, suggest that the price mechanism should not be used to encourage efficiency in the domestic sector. However, domestic energy taxation could be made acceptable if the revenue was used to give a lump sum payment to each individual, or possibly to each household. This is generally referred to as an eco-bonus, and has been the subject of extensive discussion in a number of countries. It is possible to see the eco-bonus as a forerunner to, or component of, a broader Basic Income, a proposal which has found support among a number of economists. (James Meade (1988) argued that Basic Income should be funded, in part, through environmental taxation.)

An example of how an eco-bonus might work in practice is given by Stephen Smith and Mark Pearson of the IFS (although they do not use the term). Smith and Pearson calculate that the average cost to British households of the EU carbon/energy tax would be £2.11 per week. If all the revenue collected from households was returned to them in a lump sum payments of £2.11 to each household, this would be substantially more than the extra tax paid by poor households, but much less than the extra tax paid by rich households. Thus the package overall becomes progressive. However, this does not necessarily mean that all poorer households will be better off; there may be some low-income homes with high fuel use. Pensioners, the unemployed or the ill who are at home all day clearly need more fuel than those who go to work. So an element of targeting would probably need to be built in, increasing the administrative complexity and running the risk of missing some of those most in need (Smith and Pearson, 1991).

A tax free fuel allowance
An alternative would be to give each household a tax-free fuel allowance. This would mean that only excessive use of energy would be taxed. The Dutch energy tax applies only for use above 800 cubic metres of gas and 800kWh of electricity. The notion of charging for excessive use is an approach which merits serious consideration – it could be applied to water use as well as energy. It is not in itself a guarantee against regressive impact – those groups who for the reasons mentioned have especially high fuel use may well go above the threshold. Special cases could be compensated through the benefits system – although this is subject to the concerns expressed above.

Insulation programmes
A third alternative would be to spend money insulating the homes of the poor. This should certainly be done: it would pay dividends in terms of public health and social justice as well as environmental improvement. It is the appalling state of the British housing stock which makes taxing domestic energy so regressive: these concerns simply do not exist in most other countries. Universally-available improvement grants have been withdrawn in recent years, and although there are some good schemes still in existence, such as the Home Energy Efficiency Scheme, they do not match the scale of the problem. A tax neutral package would not of course produce any extra revenue to increase spending on insulation programme. But even assuming a Government was prepared to go in for a "tax and spend" package of increasing domestic energy prices and using the revenue to upgrade the housing stock, there is an important constraint. The work should be done before any tax increase. Otherwise many poor people will be left in the cold while they wait for the extra insulation.

However, it is possible to envisage a situation in which the private sector (either energy utilities or, perhaps, building societies or others involved in property) put up the funds to carry out a programme in advance of the tax being imposed, and were recompensed from the proceeds of the tax. A scheme such as this could sensibly be administered through the Energy Savings Trust.

The Liberal Democrats have recently recommended an ingenious approach in their energy policy paper *Conserving Tomorrow*. A carbon tax would be introduced, but vouchers covering a proportion of the fuel costs would be given to those on low incomes living in badly insulated homes. These could be used either to pay a proportion of the bill, or else to pay for energy efficiency investments.

The Conservatives' imposition of VAT on domestic fuel, a blatant breach of faith with the electorate undertaken without any prior thought about compensation or measures to improve the housing stock, was rightly condemned as pernicious. Sadly, it has made sensible discussion of a non-regressive package of measures including higher domestic energy prices very difficult. It would not be impossible to design such a package, and at some stage it should be attempted. In the meantime, the case for environmental reform of the tax system needs to be decoupled from the debate about VAT on fuel. It would be straightforward to exempt the domestic sector from any further energy taxation, and this is probably the way forward. Those economists and environmentalists who argue that this means ducking the issue should remember that domestic energy taxation has increased by eight per cent. Commercial energy taxes have increased not at all.

The social impact of transport taxes
Increasing the cost of motoring is less problematic than increasing domestic energy prices. This will be a broadly progressive measure over the population as a whole, since most poor people cannot afford cars. However, it will be regressive within the car-owning community. And the fact that poor people cannot afford cars today does not mean that they do not want to be able to afford them in the future.

The impact of transport taxes is considered in detail in a paper from the IFS entitled *The Distributional Consequences of Environmental Taxes* (Johnson, McKay and Smith, 1990). The report notes that "there is a close relationship between affluence and car-ownership... The richest decile are, on average, over eleven times more likely to have the use of a car than households in the poorest decile, in which less than one household in ten has the use of a car. Moreover, households in the richer deciles are much more likely to have access to more than one car."

The IFS authors found that increasing the price of petrol by 55 pence per gallon (taking it to the highest real level it has attained over recent decades) would mean that the lowest income decile would pay an extra 0.22 per cent in tax (measured as a percentage of total spending), while the highest income decile would pay an extra 1.04 per cent. However, this happy picture is altered if one considers not all households but only those which own cars. Within this group, the lowest decile pay 1.19 per cent more in tax

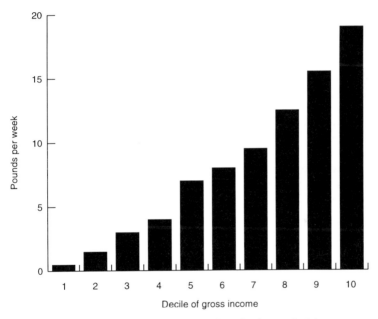

Fig 3.2 Petrol spending by household
Source: IFS

while the highest decile pay 1.07 per cent more. There will also be groups of people particularly hard hit, and they would need to be compensated. The disabled, for example, may not be in a position to benefit from better public transport. Some of the revenue from higher petrol taxes could be used to increase the disability allowance.

Those who live in rural areas inadequately served by public transport would also be adversely affected (although phasing the taxes in gradually will give these people the chance to invest in smaller, more fuel efficient vehicles). One way around this specific problem would be to invest in providing public transport alternatives in these areas, although this would depart from the principle of fiscal neutrality, and there are parts of the country which will never be adequately served by public transport. A second alternative would be to levy lower rates of tax in rural areas, although this carries the danger of so-called "tank tourism", in which urban drivers travel into the country to fill up – often quite irrationally, since they spend more on the petrol used getting there than they save from the lower cost.

A third alternative would be for central government to use some of the revenue to increase support payments to rural local authorities – possibly related to needs assessment. This need not be a departure from overall fiscal neutrality, since the local authority could then be obliged to reduce local taxation. This idea has been put forward in the past by the Liberal Democrats, and appears to be the most promising means of compensating rural dwellers without compromising the need to increase fuel prices.

We also need to consider the general argument that higher petrol taxation is only progressive because poor people cannot afford to drive – not because they do not want to. It may not damage their weekly income, but it may well damage their aspirations. Making something to which they aspire even more unattainable is hardly good social policy.

Behind this argument is the assumption that in an ideal world everyone would own or have access to a car. This is partly to do with status, but primarily because it is increasingly difficult to exist in a modern motorised society without one. Amenities are spread out over a wide area, public transport is run down, pedestrians and cyclists are too often run down also.

It does not need to be like this. Only two per cent of all journeys in the UK are made by bike, compared to ten per cent in Germany and "27 per cent in the Netherlands. Contrary to popular belief, the Dutch have not always cycled: the high levels of cycling are a result of public policy decisions made in the 1970s. Cycling rates in Germany rose by 50 per cent between 1981 and 1991. Cities such as Copenhagen, Freiburg and Groningen have shown, through extensive provision of trams, buses and cycle lanes, pedestrianisation and sensible planning policies, that it is possible to avoid or even reverse car dependency. In Freiburg, 60 per cent of journeys in 1976 were made by car; by 1992 this had fallen to 46 per cent. Walking and cycling had increased from 18 per cent to 28 per cent.

There has been a recent increase in the number of bicycles bought in the UK. The British now own fifteen million bikes. However, many of these are regarded not as a means of transport but as a leisure accessory. People drive into the country with their bikes on the back of the car rather than cycling them around the town. Better, safer cycling facilities could well reveal a latent enthusiasm for cycling among Britons.

However good the cycling tracks or public transport provision, there may still be some purposes for which a car is useful. It is easier to do the weekly or monthly shop by car, however good the public transport system (though it would not necessarily be so if supermarkets reintroduced home deliveries). People with small children may find it difficult to enjoy a holiday without a car. Access to affordable car use for such purposes – through low-cost rental services, for example – is desirable. It should be remembered that most people do not have access to a car most of the time – only around two-thirds of households have a car, and within this group there are very many families where one person drives to work and parks the car in the office car park all day, leaving the other partner to shop or transport young children by bus or train. As so often, arguments about the equity of change hides the inequity of the *status quo*.

What are the alternatives to higher petrol taxes, and would they be less regressive? One is to allow things to continue as they are, to control car use through congestion. This is highly inefficient, economically, socially and environmentally (since cars sitting in traffic jams emit a high level of pollution). As we saw earlier, it is poor communities who tend to suffer most from the resulting pollution, although British business suffers to the tune of £15–20 billion a year, the figure the CBI puts on the cost of congestion (CBI, 1995). Although road building appears to be out of favour with the public at present, failure to act on managing demand for traffic will inevitably lead to calls for an increase in the supply of roadspace. New roads will be built through the heart of communities, and these communities will not be the haunts of the well-heeled.

The easy political response is to say that congestion will be tackled through better public transport. Leaving aside the question of whether this would be enough to manage demand adequately in the absence of higher petrol prices, where in the current political climate is the money going to be found to invest in and subsidise a modern, efficient and safe public transport system? In an ideal world one might wish to increase income tax in order to fund a better transport system – as well as better education, better healthcare, better policing, better prisons, higher welfare benefits, higher overseas aid and so on. In the real world, sadly, this is not possible. Education has been identified by both Labour and the Liberal Democrats as the top priority, and (though this would come as a surprise to some members of these parties) it is possible to have only one top priority at a time. If governments do not increase their revenues, they will not have the money to increase significantly spending on public transport. Since increases in income tax and VAT do not appear to be on the agenda, to reject higher transport taxes is to accept the *status quo*, complete with congestion, pollution and road rage. Poor people might want to drive tomorrow. What they want and need today is a decent public transport system. Failing to provide one is the really regressive policy.

Unemployment and poverty

The greatest cause of poverty in Britain today is unemployment. Any package of measures which increases employment is therefore likely to be progressive. Environmental taxes might not be progressive if introduced in isolation. But if they make it possible to reduce unemployment, the net impact would be extremely positive. Green taxes would stimulate environmental industries, which in itself would create employment and improve the UK's long-term industrial prospects. And they would produce revenue, which could be used directly or indirectly to create employment. It is to the question of how to use the revenues that we now turn.

4. Recycling the revenues

The last chapter argued that governments could increase the behavioural response to environmental taxation by offering financial inducements for greener alternatives, mitigate the impact of new environmental taxes on competitiveness by reducing other taxes on business, ensure that environmental taxes were not regressive by giving low-income groups cash compensation or subsidising the services on which they depend. From this it will be clear that an environmental tax is only one half of the equation. In judging its impact and its acceptability, we have also to look at the use which is made of the revenues.

Will the revenue stream dry up?

A common criticism of environmental taxation, or at least of suggestions of how to spend the revenue, is that if the environmental tax succeeds in changing behaviour, the revenue stream will dry up. The success of the Swedish and Japanese sulphur taxes, for example, meant that the governments received much less revenue than they had expected. This could mean that taxes which had been reduced to offset new green taxes would have to be increased again in the medium term.

Representative of this train of thought is the following paragraph by John Hills of the LSE on the subject of taxing "bads" such as pollution:

> There may indeed be compelling microeconomic efficiency reasons for any of these taxes on the grounds that the market does not give producers and consumers the right signals, so that imposing a tax "internalises" what would otherwise be an external cost or benefit. But it is a great mistake to assume that they constitute a painless way of boosting government revenues or substituting for other taxes. If they are really successful in curbing some undesirable activity, they raise no revenue. In order to sell them politically, they may have to be tied to compensation (as with VAT on domestic fuel) or an equivalent reduction in some other tax on the same group (as with the landfill levy) so again, little net revenue may result. If only some people or businesses change behaviour, revenue is raised, but the

history of the extension of VAT to domestic fuel should disabuse
people of the idea that taxing "bads" is going to be painless.

(Hills, 1996)

The final point is certainly a good one, and there is little doubt that policy
makers have been suitably disabused. But the paragraph contains a
contradiction and an oversimplification. Hills argues that environmental
taxes cannot be used as substitutes for other taxes. But he goes on to point
out that the landfill tax is to be matched by a reduction in another tax on
the same group. This will indeed result in "little net revenue". But the
revenue will now be coming from a tax which increases efficiency rather
than one which distorts the labour market; surely a worthwhile reform, and
just the type of substitution which Hills says is not possible. The
oversimplification lies in the claim that a tax which succeeds in changing
behaviour will not increase revenues. This is true only if the change in
behaviour is total, if the activity in question is wholly eliminated. There are
some environmental issues where this is the desired outcome; the use of
CFCs, for example. But we argued earlier that in such cases regulation
would be a more sensible policy tool. In most cases, what is required is
simply that we use less of something – energy, transport, aggregates – not
that we stop using it altogether.

One can draw a distinction between activities which are liable to be highly
price responsive, and for which alternatives exist, so that ultimately they will
cease altogether, and activities which will simply continue at a lower level.
Examples of the first include the use of chlorine – in Sweden, even a
discussion of a tax was enough to prompt industry to phase out its use
altogether (Sterner, 1994) – or the use of some products such as heavy-metal
batteries. But both energy and transport must fall into the second category.
However high the price, society will not cease to need energy and transport.

Most sensible proposals for environmental taxes suggest phasing the new tax
in gradually. This means that government revenues can be maintained or
even increased in the face of falling use. Consider the example of an
industrial energy tax. Pre-tax, industry uses 1000 units of energy, at a cost of
£20 per unit (these figures are purely indicative). Industry's energy bill is
therefore £20,000, and government revenues are zero. A tax of £1 per unit
is then imposed. If the initial behavioural effect is to reduce energy use by
five per cent, energy use will be 950 units, industry's energy bill will be
virtually unchanged at £19,950 and revenue to the government £950. In the
next year the tax is doubled to £2 per unit, and energy use falls to 900 units.
Industry's energy bill is now £19,800, and government revenues are £1,800.

And so on. The net result is that industry pays almost the same for its total energy use, but uses less, benefiting the environment. There is no reason why output should fall; as we have seen, there is considerable scope to increase the efficiency with which energy is used. The government has a new stream of revenue. The only loser is the energy supply industry.

Of course the process cannot continue indefinitely. At some point industry will be unable to reduce energy use any further, or it will be prohibitively expensive to do so. Further increases in the rate of taxation would then translate into increased burdens on industry. What governments should seek is this new equilibrium, at which the economy is operating in a more efficient and sustainable manner without any impact on profitability or competitiveness, and the Treasury is making some money into the bargain.

It will always be difficult to predict where this equilibrium will be. There will be errors in predicting the reaction to environmental taxes, and thus how great the revenues will be. But predicting the public finances is hardly an exact science today, as John Hills recognises. Indeed, in 1992 Treasury estimates for the coming year were £11 billion out (Hills,1996). There is no reason why revenues from environmental taxation should be any less predictable than current taxes on employment, consumer spending and the like.

Taxes on products or practices which are likely to disappear altogether should be regarded as a finite revenue source; they could perhaps be used to fund specific, time-limited programmes aimed at speeding up the resolution of the environmental problem – tax credits or subsidies for particular pollution abatement equipment, for example. Taxes on generic and essential activities – energy use, transport, waste disposal – can be regarded as providing a secure, indefinite revenue stream, and the receipts can, if a government so desires, be used to reduce other taxes.

The tobacco tax problem

However, a further objection arises. If a Government receives revenue from something, it will have a strong incentive to encourage it in order to maximise its receipts. This sort of "fiscal addiction" is generally referred to as the tobacco tax problem.

There is no neat or easy answer to this. One has to accept that by introducing green taxes one is placing temptation in the path of future Chancellors. And the fact that successive Governments have refused to ban tobacco advertising, despite overwhelming evidence of its damaging impact, suggests that narrow revenue-raising concerns can overpower broader and more enlightened thoughts. The Government's unwillingness to manage demand for transport may also be related to the revenue it receives from car drivers (it is also, obviously, related to the votes it receives from them). Indeed, Kenneth Clarke is reported to have been the most vociferous Cabinet opponent of the Royal Commission's Report on Transport and the Environment.

But the fact that governments have a temptation to behave badly does not mean, inevitably, that they will behave badly. All governments raise revenue from tobacco taxes, yet some have banned tobacco advertising, including Italy and France. All governments also raise money from motorists, but some do try to restrain traffic growth. One should not assume that all British governments will be stupid and short-sighted.

Arguably, the extra cost to the National Health Service of smoking-related illness may well outweigh the extra revenue the Treasury receives from the refusal to ban advertising. British industry also pays a price, in terms of absenteeism and reduced productivity. The same points can be made about the failure to tackle pollution. The National Asthma Campaign has calculated, for example, that this disease alone costs the NHS £450 million, with total costs to British industry of £1 billion a year.

The way to ensure that a government does not succumb to fiscal addiction is to maintain public pressure for responsible policies – this has largely been achieved with smoking (the banning of advertising will be the culmination) and progress is at last being made on transport. Institutional changes could also help: a Department of Health which promoted public well-being rather than administering to the sick; a Department of the Environment which included transport and energy under its aegis (though it is wishful thinking in the UK context to assume that either would be able to overrule the Treasury).

Fiscal addiction is a potential problem. But it would be unduly pessimistic to reject environmental taxation on these grounds. The temptation can be reduced by countervailing pressures. And even if a government does succumb, it is not clear that the resulting situation will be worse for health or the environment than a situation with no taxes and a virtuous government. Would fewer people smoke if cigarettes were untaxed but all tobacco advertising was banned? Would fewer people drive if petrol was untaxed but the government enthusiastically promoted public transport? It seems very unlikely. Price generally has more impact on behaviour than exhortation does.

Use of revenues from existing green taxes

How do governments use the revenues from existing environmental taxes? In most cases they are treated as part of the general pool – this is true of all the "environmental" taxes in the UK (although the landfill tax has been linked, presentationally at least, with reductions in labour taxes, as we shall see). Some public expenditure is used to promote environmental goals, by subsidising public transport, clean energy generation, research into pollution abatement and so on. Investment incentives are also widely used; for example, France has enhanced depreciation allowances for investments which benefit the environment. Since some money is being raised from green taxes, and some money spent on green programmes, a linkage could be said to exist. But it is not generally formalised.

However, in some cases revenues are hypothecated to particular environmental purposes. For example:

● Ninety-five per cent of the revenue raised by explicitly environmental charges in France is earmarked to national or regional agencies, while the money raised through motorway tolls is given to motorway companies.

● The revenues from Catalonia's waste water charges, (around £100 million in 1993) are used to invest in new treatment plants.

● The revenues from the US tax on chemical feedstock are given to the Environmental Protection Agency to help clean up contaminated land.

● The revenues from Sweden's tax on domestic flights are invested in railway infrastructure to encourage the switch from air to rail.

● The revenues from Sweden's battery charges are used to finance collection and safe disposal of used batteries.

● One of the more imaginative uses of revenue is the Saskatchewan packaging tax. The funds from this are used to employ in recycling centres people with disabilities who would otherwise probably be unemployed.

Revenues are generally only hypothecated to environmental programmes if they are not very substantial. Revenues from Dutch fuel taxes used to be hypothecated to environmental policy expenditures, but were allocated to the central Exchequer in 1992 – mainly because they had increased very substantially.

Should revenues be hypothecated?

Some have argued that hypothecation would be a good means of building public support for new or increased taxes. Mulgan and Murray (1993), for example, argue for "a return to hypothecation as a way of restoring people's sense of connection". They suggest that it would reduce central budgetary control (which they regard as a plus), stimulate more informed public debate about priorities, and increase legitimacy.

There is a difference between formal and presentational hypothecation. It may be that all that is needed is more presentational hypothecation: "we are putting this tax up so that we can fund that". Governments do this all the time – for example, the increase in VAT to 17.5 per cent was linked to subsidies to local authorities to reduce the poll tax. The Liberal Democrat proposal to increase income tax by 1p in order to fund an increase in education expenditure is an example of informal or presentational earmarking.

However, people may well not believe the government, and they may doubt that in the absence of formal hypothecation future revenues will be earmarked for the same use. Mulgan and Murray argue for formal hypothecation. Would this be a sensible way of building public support for green taxes? In some cases the answer is probably yes. Spending revenues in environmentally-related fields will often increase the behavioural response to a tax, and so increase the environmental benefit. So in some cases, a package of measures including a tax and directly-related expenditures will be appropriate. Hypothecation should therefore be considered whenever a new tax is proposed.

However, we are sceptical of hypothecation as a general principle. There are some familiar and well-rehearsed political objections (for example, would people not using the service being funded be allowed an opt out from the tax?) which cast doubt on the claim that it would necessarily increase legitimacy. More fundamentally, we are not convinced that it would produce more debate about priorities, nor that the weakening of central budgetary control is desirable.

Consider the case of road pricing. It is often asserted that it should only be introduced if the revenues are hypothecated to public transport investments; this is the position taken by the Liberal Democrats, for example. Yet this would be a means of restricting local authority freedom. Why should a local authority not be able to introduce road pricing in order to increase funding for its schools or its old people's homes? The reason for the emergence of elected, multi-purpose authorities to replace single-issue boards was precisely to enable localities to decide between options and priorities. Without hypothecation, an authority can decide its spending priorities year by year (leaving aside the question of central control). With hypothecation, it is seriously restricted. It cannot decide to give priority to education if most of its revenues come from transport. It could, in theory, reduce its transport taxes and increase whatever it was that funded schools. But the road pricing might be having a beneficial effect on traffic management – it might not want to reduce the tax. So local authorities with state-of-the-art public transport systems and shoddy schools could emerge. This is not sensible.

The same could be true at national level if, say, revenues from higher fuel duties were hypothecated to intercity railways. A country could end up with too many high speed rail links and too few hospitals. Weakening central government control over local government may be desirable, but weakening the capacity of either central or local government to choose between competing priorities is not.

Hypothecation should always be considered for the revenues from any new or increased green tax: in some cases it will be appropriate. But in general public authorities should retain flexibility to decide between competing priorities, thus maximising the scope for democratic choice.

Green tax reform

A government needing to increase its tax revenues, for whatever reason, would be well advised to make greater use of green taxes rather than other options. They will raise revenue in a less distorting way, and help achieve environmental goals to boot. However, it is important to disentangle the arguments for more (or less) tax from the arguments for different taxes. Whatever the level of taxation, it is sensible to raise revenue as efficiently as possible.

Current fiscal systems often raise money in an inefficient and illogical way. As the Delors White Paper on *Growth, Competitiveness and Employment* puts it:

> The current development model in the Community is...
> characterised by an insufficient use of labour resources and an
> excessive use of natural resources, and results in a deterioration in the
> quality of life.
>
> (European Commission, 1993b)

What is needed, according to Delors, is a new "sustainable development model" which will shift the trajectory of economic development, breaking the link between economic growth and environmental degradation, ending the squandering of natural resources and the waste of human talent. Reforming the tax system could help make this shift.

Across the EU, roughly fifty per cent of all taxes are levied directly or indirectly on labour (mainly through income tax and social security contributions), and less than ten per cent on natural resources. The burden of taxation on labour has increased steadily (from around 30 per cent in 1960), while that on natural resources has actually declined (European Commission, 1993a). (There is controversy among economists about the extent to which differences in the formal incidence of taxation affect the actual incidence: some argue that taxes on energy end up as taxes on labour anyway. This argument is considered in the next section.)

One reason for the imbalance is that despite the single European market and its emphasis on the right of workers to move freely between member states, labour remains a relatively immobile factor of production, unlike capital which moves easily from country to country. Governments therefore prefer to tax labour. But there is increasing concern in states which have used labour taxes to finance welfare about the impact on employment and on competitiveness.

However, there is little scope for dramatic reductions in expenditure – even eighteen years of Conservative government in the UK, committed to cutting back the activities of the state and not overly concerned with the impact on welfare recipients, have resulted in public spending which is essentially unchanged as a percentage of GDP. So significant reductions in non-wage labour costs would need to be matched by tax increases elsewhere. And since, as we saw in chapters one and two, there is a strong rationale for environmental taxation, an obvious package of reforms emerges.

A recent paper by the European Commissioner responsible for the Single Market, Mario Monti, argues that while governments have maintained overall levels of tax revenue, this "has been achieved at the cost of a progressive alteration in the structure of taxation; the tax burden has been shifted to the less mobile tax base – labour – in order to recover the tax lost from the erosion of other more mobile bases". The paper recommends a shift away from labour taxes to VAT, property taxes and green taxes (European Commission, 1996). The OECD has recommended the same course of action.

The Business Council for Sustainable Development, an umbrella body including senior figures from Dow, Du Pont, Volkswagen, Ciba-Geigy, Mitsubishi and several other large corporations, has published a report arguing that:

> Switching some of the revenue burden from taxes on income, employment and profits to environmental charges on resource waste would yield double benefits. Net savings would occur from the reduced cost of environmental protection and reduced environmental damages... The new "eco-balance" would shift tax receipts away from wages. It would encourage new investments in cleaner technologies by allowing for the expansion of investment opportunities, and reduce the tax disincentive on labour, thereby creating jobs and reducing unemployment"
>
> (BCSD 1994)

The claim, as this indicates, is that lowering labour costs and increasing environmental taxes would deliver a "double dividend" of a better environment and higher employment. If energy or raw materials are considered as production inputs whose use is to be minimised, an obvious use of the revenue from taxing them is to make cheaper another, substitute input by cutting labour taxes.

Considerable work has been done to try to demonstrate the possibility of a double dividend through econometric modelling. The European Commission (1992a) suggests that its carbon/energy tax would reduce energy consumption by 2.8 per cent after seven years. The biggest impact would be on industrial demand, which would fall by 4.8 per cent. Using the revenues to make a one per cent general reduction in employers social security contributions would mean that, again after seven years, both employment and GDP would be one per cent higher than in the base case (European Commission, 1993a).

The impact of a broader tax reform package, including a carbon/energy tax, higher transport taxes, agricultural input taxes, and water taxes as well as a range of non-fiscal measures, has been modelled for the European Commission by a consortium of consultants led by DRI. They too predict that if employers' social security contributions were reduced, GDP would be one per cent higher than in the reference case. Employment is predicted to be 2.2 million higher by 2010, reducing the unemployment rate by one per cent (DRI, 1994).

The impact of the carbon/energy tax plus reductions in employers social security contributions on six member states is modelled in a paper presented at an OECD conference in 1994. This predicts effects on employment as follows: Germany, up 0.79 per cent; France, up 0.44 per cent; UK, up 0.56 per cent; Italy, up 0.79 per cent; Netherlands, up 0.3 per cent; Belgium, up 0.88 per cent (Majocchi, 1994).

The Deutsches Institut fur Wirtschaftung carried out a study into the impact of a unilateral green tax reform in Germany, involving progressively rising energy taxes leading after ten years to a 24 per cent increase in the price of petrol, a 46 per cent increase for household electricity and a 96 per cent increase for industrial electricity. There would be an increase in employment of 600,000, and insignificant impacts on economic growth and competitiveness. Energy use declines by 7 per cent. (DIW, 1994).

A study by Erasme modelled the impact of a carbon/energy tax in France, with the receipts used for: financial incentives towards energy conservation, for both households and industry (16 per cent of total receipts); lowering VAT on non-energy intensive goods (53 per cent); lowering employers' national insurance (31 per cent). This package is regarded as having the best macro-economic and environmental effect, reducing carbon dioxide emissions by 13.4 per cent and creating 90,000 new jobs (Bureau du Plan-Erasme, 1993).

Is there really a double dividend?

Although the proposal that we should tax "bads" rather than "goods" seems common sense there is no agreement among economists that a tax switch of the kind proposed would do much for employment. Indeed, some economists have argued that the double dividend would prove a mirage. But they tend to base their arguments on particular assumptions which are, at best, questionable. As Nicholas Mabey of the London Business School puts it:

> The potential for positive output effects from recycling carbon taxes
> is contentious, as some theoretical economic models deny such an

effect is possible. These negative results are usually driven by an initial assumption that the labour market clears at a given wage and existing mixes of taxation are roughly optimal (Mabey, 1995).

Some of those sceptical of the double dividend argue that employers do not pay labour taxes anyway; the tax burden is generally all shifted onto wages. The theoretical reason why this might be true is that capital is more mobile internationally than labour, so that it will tend to move from a jurisdiction in which labour is highly taxed. This will eventually lead to a fall in real wages in that jurisdiction, so that the total cost of labour (wages plus labour taxes) is equal to the total cost of labour in its competitors. The empirical evidence on this is not conclusive, but data from different countries in Europe does tend to support the proposition. Most of the variation in non-wage labour costs (which is substantial) is offset by differences in take-home pay.

On this view, it does not matter whether firms are taxed on labour or energy: the real wage takes the strain either way. A shift in taxation from labour to energy will have little or no impact on the real take-home wage. It does not follow, however, that it will have no effect on employment. The fact that the tax switch is revenue-neutral leaves overall unit production costs unchanged, but it alters the relative price of factors. Firms will be able to increase profits if they can arrange to use more labour and less energy.

The crucial assumption which makes some economists question the double dividend is that a reduction in non-wage labour costs might well increase the demand for labour in the short run, but in the long run the increased demand for labour would raise wages, causing employment to fall again. Whether or not this is true depends on how the labour market works. The orthodox view is that nominal wages are set by a bargaining process which determines an equilibrium unemployment rate, known as the non-accelerating-inflation rate of unemployment or NAIRU. Underlying the bargaining, in the orthodox view, the potential supply of labour is almost fixed. As labour demand rises, unemployment may initially fall below the NAIRU, but – so the orthodox story goes – nominal wages will accelerate. Firms will attempt to pass on these higher costs into prices but so long as monetary policy is not accommodating they will be unable to do so. Hence the real wage will rise and labour demand will fall. Once again the effect will be felt on the real wage, not on unemployment.

The trouble with this story is that it seems to describe a world that no-one can recognise. To the non-economist it seems clear enough that the UK, in common with most other European countries, has large numbers of unemployed people who would be prepared to work at existing average wages or even less if a job were available. If we drop the orthodox assumptions of an inelastic labour supply, the tax switch can raise employment in both the short and the long term.

Initially, faced with higher energy taxes and lower wage costs, the firm has an incentive to move to a more labour-intensive, less energy-intensive form of production. Doing so may require new investment. As this investment takes place over time, the growth in employment is higher than it would otherwise have been, and the growth in energy consumption is lower. If there is an elastic labour supply, then higher labour demand bids nominal wages up, but this calls forth more workers into the labour market. Employment rises, though unemployment does not necessarily fall. Inflation need not, therefore, accelerate.

The outcome could be even better: since a rise in labour demand could initially reduce unemployment (before the increase in the supply of labour takes effect), the NAIRU itself could fall a little – a phenomenon known as hysteresis. There would then be a permanent reduction in the unemployment rate, though small in relation to the rise in employment.

A variation on the fixed labour-supply assumption puts the blame on trade unions. There may be unemployed people about, but if the total cost of labour has fallen, due to reductions in labour taxes, trade unions may feel able to demand higher wages, on the grounds that employers are now in a position to pay more, particularly in sectors where energy use is low. The increase in employment could therefore be contingent on pay restraint among the already-employed. This has led some supporters of reform to talk in terms of "social contracts" with trade unions being necessary to ensure that the benefits will not be dissipated. Some Dutch trade unions have agreed not to press for wage rises following the limited tax reform there. However, trade unions will not necessarily have any greater bargaining power, since the rate of unemployment will not have fallen substantially. And the decline in union coverage, combined with changes in employment law, would weaken the capacity of British unions to react in this way, even assuming they wanted to. There is therefore no reason to assume that the all the reduction in labour costs will be mopped up by higher wage claims – though some if it may be.

A final reason advanced to question the double dividend is that companies may fail to react to the reduction in labour taxes by increasing demand for labour. This possibility depends on how far they can economise on now-more-expensive energy without employing more workers.

All of these considerations mean that there could be lower gains in employment than the models predict. However, this is not a strong argument against tax reform. Market mechanisms will in many cases be the most efficient way to meet environmental goals. Offsetting reductions in other taxes are required to ensure that the package is not inflationary and does not damage overall competitiveness. One dividend, the environmental one, would be reason enough to proceed, provided that there were not economic penalties. The academic dispute is about the size of the "windfall" gain in employment; no one appears to believe that the impact on employment will be negative. Short-term reductions in unemployment are still worthwhile – and in this case short term might mean a number of years. And higher wages, although they may reduce the increase in employment, are not in themselves undesirable.

Targeting labour tax reductions

In one respect there is much more widespread agreement that lowering non-wage labour costs will increase employment. A NIC reduction would make much more difference to the employment equation at the lower end of the scale than at the higher end (no one is going to employ an extra City economist because the NIC rate has been cut a couple of percent). It is generally accepted that at the bottom of the labour market, the low-wage, unskilled end, the supply of labour is likely to be elastic. People whose spouses are in work, for example, may be quite sensitive to the wages they are paid in making the decision to join the paid labour force or stay at home. A targeted reduction of wage costs at the bottom end is highly likely to lead to more employment. The costs are a higher proportion of the total remuneration of the low paid anyway so firms are more likely to react at that end of the market as costs fall. In practice, therefore, the tax switch is likely to lead to more employment, perhaps a lot more employment, but we should expect most of it to be at the lower end of the pay spectrum.

A good summary of the way in which even those sceptical of the link between NICs and employment accept the likelihood of job creation at the lower end of the pay scale is provided by the Employment Policy Institute:

> Most research on NWLCs [Non-Wage Labour Costs] indicates that employers "backshift" NWLCs onto employees. Nickell and Bell (1995), for example, find that there is no significant relationship between unit labour costs and payroll taxes because payroll taxes are ultimately shifted onto employees. Countries with similar levels of productivity and similar labour costs show great differences in the

share of NWLCs. Denmark is often cited as the classic case of an EU country where payroll taxes are minimal but where total labour costs are no lower than elsewhere. Jackman, Layard and Nickell (1996), having examined all the available evidence, find that while changes in payroll taxes can exert short-run effects on wage costs and jobs, wages subsequently adjust. They thus conclude that such taxes "do not appear to have any long-term effect on unemployment". However, this general conclusion about the effects of NWLCs on employment may not apply to low skilled workers. Although wages in general adjust in the long-term to changes in NWLCs, the same may not be true for low-wage, low-productivity workers whose wages tend to be more downwardly rigid. Where it is impossible to shift the burden of payroll taxes fully onto employees – because minimum wages or benefit payments serve to set a floor on wages – a cut in NWLCs in therefore likely to encourage more job creation (Employment Policy Institute, 1996).

The European Commission has modelled the impact of targeting the cuts in employers' contributions to the low paid. This leads to more positive employment benefits: employment rises by 2.2 per cent rather than one per cent. Using the revenue saved due to the drop in unemployment to make further cuts in social security taxes leads to an increase in employment of three per cent – 6.6 million extra jobs across the Community (European Commission, 1993a).

If it is desired to create higher skilled jobs, targeting of low-paid NICs could be combined with a training subsidy for the same workers (although this could not of course be financed out of a tax neutral reform package). Such refinements go beyond the scope of this study, but are central to the questions of how to tackle unemployment (see Holtham and Mayhew (1996) for further consideration of policies to address long-term unemployment).

Alternative uses for the revenue

Cutting labour taxes is not, of course, the only way in which revenue from green taxes could be recycled into the economy – it is not hard to think of ways to disburse several billion pounds of public money, either through higher spending or through tax cuts. Essentially this is a political decision. However, the choice should be subject to certain considerations. In particular, the decision should depend in part on the nature of the revenue stream. If it is predicted that the reaction to the new tax will be a significant change in behaviour, so that the revenue will diminish quickly and perhaps even disappear, it would not be appropriate to reduce other taxes. As argued in chapter four, some of the revenue could be used to offer inducements to environmental investment to reduce the pollutant in question, since this expenditure would be similarly finite. These could be part of a mutuality package if fiscal neutrality is desired.

Where the revenue stream is secure – for example with motoring taxes, waste taxes or energy taxes – offsetting tax reductions can be considered, but they are not the only option. There is always the option of using some of the revenue to increase public spending or reduce borrowing. Using revenue from green taxes to pay for other environmentally-related policies might be helpful in building public support. For example, revenues from road pricing could be used to invest in or subsidise public transport; energy taxes could be used to offer subsidies for research into new energy efficiency or renewable generation technologies; taxes on toxic emissions to water, air or soil could fund a clean-up of the water environment or contaminated land. If taxing pollution now and thereby reducing it in the future yields a revenue surplus, it seems consistent to use the surplus to undo the consequences of past pollution.

More generally, there is a strong case for increasing public expenditure on policies which promote the development of environmental technologies – this should be regarded as a form of investment in Britain's industrial future. The United States spends $4 billion a year (over £2.5 billion) on environmental R&D; Japan spends 52 billion yen (£325 million). Britain spends only £40-50 million (depending on exact definitions). If well spent, the money could yield a positive return over time, to the public finances as well as to the economy.

If job creation is the priority, it is likely that there are more cost-effective means of creating jobs than reducing labour taxes. Cambridge Econometrics predicts that every £1 billion used to reduce employers' NICs will produce just 17,000 new jobs, a cost-per-job of £58,000. This compares with estimates as low as £3,000 per job for purpose-designed schemes to tackle long-term unemployment (Holtham and Mayhew, 1996). In addition, it is unlikely that reducing labour taxes will address the problem of the long-term unemployed: a more direct approach will be needed for this. Direct job-creation schemes could again be linked to environmental goals – a national programme of energy efficiency could create tens of thousands of jobs as well as cutting energy wastage and addressing the fuel poverty – thus building public support for the new environmental taxes.

A Government seeking to increase the tax taken to finance these or other measures should look first to environmental taxation, the least distorting form of taxation and one which will also contribute to broader public policy goals. However, we are working in this paper on an assumption of tax neutrality. We want to focus the argument on how revenue is raised, not how much is raised. The aim is to shift the burden of taxation, so that the system works in a more efficient, less perverse and more sustainable way. The scale of the revenues which could be raised through environmental taxes is substantial – a commercial energy tax alone could raise several billion pounds. It is not necessary or desirable to postpone the greening of the tax system until a consensus emerges for a higher overall level of taxation.

Moreover, tax reductions will be necessary to compensate industry and individuals for increased costs. Although some of the green tax increase will be avoided though reduced use of energy, less waste being produced or other adjustments, the new environmental taxes we propose would, *ceteris paribus*, lead to increases in business costs. This would have two effects. In the non-traded sector, higher prices would be fed through to the consumer, leading to a cut in real wages and, perhaps, inflationary pressures. In the traded sector, there would be a loss of competitiveness. Tax reductions would be needed to offset both effects. Where should such tax cuts be made?

Cuts in personal taxation will appeal strongly to politicians. But one should be wary of using too much of the revenue from environmental taxes to cut income tax or VAT. Much of the impact of new taxes will fall on business, and if an inflationary spiral is to be avoided, and competitiveness protected, most of the offsetting reductions should go to business too. In Sweden the initial tax reform package involved reductions in income tax and increases in energy tax. Business was therefore not compensated for its increased costs. Strong and sustained industrial lobbying led to a reform of the reform, after only one year, in which industrial energy taxes were reduced.

Reductions in personal taxation would also probably be relatively ineffective at creating jobs: certainly this is true of cuts in income tax, although cuts in VAT have had a better press among analysts. A European Commission study (European Commission, 1992b) considered the impact of reducing income tax or VAT, rather than employers' social security contributions. If income tax is reduced, the model predicts that there will be an initial positive effect, but a slight decline in employment because the consumption boom leads to more inflation. If VAT is reduced, inflationary pressures are avoided, but there is a predicted increase in employment of just 0.1 per cent, compared to one per cent if employers' social security contributions are reduced.

Reductions in personal taxation, if they are deemed necessary for political reasons, should be confined to the revenues which fall directly on individuals, such as motoring taxes. There is also a case for an increase in revenue support grant to local authorities, to compensate for increased waste disposal charges. This would avoid an increase in Council Tax. But most of the revenue should be used to reduce business taxation.

A simple option would be to reduce corporation tax. However, the marginal rate in the UK is already quite low by international standards and does not seem to be an impediment to inward investment. There is not much political gain in proposing reductions.

One of the main problems with increasing business costs is that it would reduce cash flow available for investment. There are certain features of the UK corporate tax system which already militate against investment. Green tax revenues could be used meet the costs of a tax reform aimed at eliminating those biases. In essence, the bias comes from two phenomena. One is that while interest payments on finance raised for investment are tax deductible, no similar allowance is made for the return to equity finance. Giving firms such an allowance would cost billions of pounds. The second feature is the regime for taxing dividends, under which tax-exempt investors such as pension funds receive cash payments from the Exchequer to top up their dividend receipts – these are to compensate for the corporation tax paid by companies in respect of those dividends. Since tax-exempt institutions now hold a majority of shares in UK companies, this system creates a bias in favour of profit distribution. If companies received an allowance for equity capital, logically there would be no repayments of tax to institutional investors, ending this bias. Even so, the net cost of a reform would be several billion pounds a year.

Such a reform would certainly be preferable to *ad hoc* changes in investment allowances. There may be more of a case for targeted investment allowances. In Japan there are 18 per cent tax incentives for investments in pollution abatement equipment, and up to 30 per cent tax credits for environmental R&D. In France there are accelerated depreciation provisions for investments which benefit the environment. (Opschoor and Voss, 1989). In Germany the costs of investment in pollution-abatement equipment can be set against the costs of water discharge charges. There is also DM 4.3 billion a year of low-interest loans available for environmental investments. This would be a sensible use of some of the money, particularly where the revenue stream is not expected to last long (the investment credits and loans can be withdrawn once all or most of the pollution is abated).

An alternative option which deserves serious considerations is to use some of the revenue to reduce business rates. The debate about business rates in recent years has focused on whether they should be controlled nationally or locally. This has obscured the fact that business rates are an illogical tax. They bear no relation to the performance or profitability of a company – the same must be paid in good years and bad. Many companies which might otherwise survive go under because a downturn in business leaves them unable to afford their rates. Indeed business rates are identified by small businesses as one of the greatest causes for concern.

Small businesses may be particularly affected by increases in environmental taxation. Larger companies are likely to have a dedicated environmental manager who can identify efficiency improvements and thus tax minimisation. Small companies are less likely to have the expertise, or the personnel able to acquire it. There would thus be merit in targeting some of the offsetting tax reductions which will particularly benefit this sector, by reducing business rates.

Green tax reform in practice

The debate about environmental tax reform has been around for many years, although it is relatively muted in Britain. Predictably, it is the Scandinavian countries which have progressed furthest towards implementation – the trend has now spread south to the Netherlands, with Austria and Switzerland set to follow.

Sweden introduced a major tax reform in 1990 and 1991, resulting in a significant redistribution of the tax burden (representing six per cent of GDP). The main concern was to reduce the very high rates of personal income tax – the top rate, including social security contributions, was 80 per cent. In 1991, the standard rate was cut to 30 per cent, and the top rate to 50 per cent. Excise taxes on some luxuries were abolished, and capital taxes simplified and made more uniform. At the same time, the tax bases for income tax and VAT were broadened, the rate of VAT increased, and new energy taxes introduced.

The tax reform in Norway also took place over a two-year period. In 1991, a range of environmental taxes was introduced, including sulphur and carbon taxes. In 1992 the rates of personal and company taxation were lowered.

Denmark implemented a reform package in 1993, reducing income taxes and increasing environmental taxes on households. In 1996 the "Danish Energy Package" extended CO_2 and energy taxes to industry and introduced a sulphur tax. Revenue will be recycled primarily through reduced employers' social security contributions. However, some will be used for investment incentives, and some will be targeted at the small business sector.

In January 1996 the Netherlands introduced a carbon/energy tax on small energy users: households and small commercial establishments. The revenue will be used to reduce direct taxes.

Prospects for green tax reform

The German government had been thought to be sympathetic to the concept of environmental tax reform, and the CDU has had a number of parliamentary working groups considering specific proposals (as have all the other parties). However, a recent (1996) paper from the German Finance Ministry suggests that movement is not imminent – it argues that green taxes may not be effective in protecting the environment, and that it will be difficult to predict the revenues. However, the Government remains committed to achieving a ratio of 50/50 between direct and indirect taxes, and in 1995 the ration was 54 per cent direct to 46 per cent indirect. So four per cent of total tax revenues need to be shifted, which means that environmental taxation may yet be increased, to allow for reductions in direct taxes.

A number of leading German companies, including AEG, Frosch and Tupperware, have come out in support of green tax reform, running full page advertisements demanding that politicians "put this long-overdue tax reform into practice". The German trade union federation, the Deutscher Gewerkschaftsbund (DGB) has called for "the introduction of a general energy tax on all fossil fuels and electricity (with the exception of electricity generated from renewable sources), as a first step towards an ecological tax reform". It would like if possible a co-ordinated EU-wide tax, but does not regard this as a precondition. (DGB, 1995)

The Italian Government announced a comprehensive tax reform package in December 1994 which, as well as reducing labour taxes and increasing energy ones, aimed to simplify tax structures, reducing the number of statutes from over 100 to under 20. Half a million copies of a White Paper called *From People to Things* were distributed in order to stimulate a wide public debate.

The Berlusconi Government fell soon after the publication of the White Paper. The Government of Lamberto Dini which took over did not take up the proposals; it is too soon to say whether the new Left Government will take any interest.

The debate in the UK

The concept of a green tax reform is not nearly as widely debated in the UK as in many other European countries, but it has been gaining support gradually in recent years. Conservative Chancellor Kenneth Clarke signed up to the principle when he linked the new landfill tax to a reduction in employers' National Insurance Contributions, saying: "I want to increase the tax on polluters, and make further cuts in the tax on jobs". (The Treasury subsequently pointed out that this was not hypothecation but a presentational link – a future Chancellor is not obliged to put any extra revenues from the landfill tax into reducing NICs). However, the landfill tax raises a comparatively small amount of money, around half a million pounds a year, so the shift cannot be said to be significant, and the 1995 Budget contained no new taxes on polluters.

A number of Government Advisory bodies have supported the principle of environmental tax reform. The Panel on Sustainable Development, set up by John Major after the Rio Summit to advise him on environmental matters, has called for "wider use of economic instruments, and a gradual move away from taxes on labour, income, profits and capital towards taxes on pollution and the use of resources, including energy". The Advisory Committee on Business and the Environment (ACBE), which includes representatives from major energy, construction, retailing and financial services companies, has stated that "ACBE welcomed the Chancellor's statement in his 1994 Budget that in future the Government would be looking to shift the burden of taxation from wealth creation to resource use and pollution".

Environmental groups have mostly overcome earlier scepticism about green taxes and many, including Friends of the Earth and the RSPB, now campaign in favour of green tax reform. The recently launched Real World Coalition, which brings together environmental and social policy groups (itself a significant development) strongly supports a tax shift (Jacobs, 1996).

Although the Left has traditionally resisted the notion that the cost of labour contributes to unemployment, it is becoming increasingly widely accepted that labour costs – and in particular non-wage labour costs – should be reduced in order to encourage employers to create more jobs. For example, the report of the Commission on Social Justice calls for:

> The development of a tax and benefits system which provides incentives, not disincentives, to employment. This will require ... gradual reduction in taxes on employment, particularly for less-skilled and lower-paid jobs (Commission on Social Justice, 1994).

The Labour Party, in its 1994 Environment Policy Statement *In Trust for Tomorrow*, commits itself to:

> a long term, gradual change to the way in which the economy is organised, to ensure that it encourages "goods" such as employment, value added, investment and savings, and discourages "bads" such as pollution and resource depletion.

This sounds encouraging. But the language is hardly indicative of firm commitment, and a pledge to encourage good things cannot really be described as a radical policy innovation. The Liberal Democrats have committed themselves to a phased introduction of a carbon tax on energy production, with safeguards for domestic consumers. Renewables would be exempted. Revenues would be recycled to reduce other taxes – these are not specified.

Some concern has been expressed by trade unionists about the weakening of the contributory principle if employers' National Insurance Contributions are reduced (although it is perhaps worth remembering that radical trade unions opposed the introduction of National Insurance when Lloyd George proposed it in 1911, arguing that benefits should be paid out of general taxation). The contributory principle is a fiction – National Insurance Contributions are not nearly large enough to cover what they are supposed to fund. The notion that employers should take responsibility for some aspects of their employees' well-being is a noble sentiment, and in an age of full employment or labour scarcity would be worthy of strong support. Sadly, in an age of mass unemployment when public policy makers need in effect to induce employers to take on more workers, it appears something of a luxury. What matters to individuals, in this context, is that they have a job and that there is a decent welfare system. The way in which the revenue is raised to finance the welfare system is surely a second order concern, and it must be sensible to organise the tax system in a way which maximises employment.

In any case, opposition to reductions in employers' NICs should not be taken as opposition to the concept of green tax reform, only as opposition to one variant of it. The revenues could equally be used to cut income tax, business rates, corporation tax or VAT.

Overall, the debate in the UK is slowly widening, and there are some influential voices supporting reform. However, it is much easier to sign up to a principle than to support and implement specific reform packages. We need now to move beyond the theory and discuss practicalities. The next chapter considers options for new or increased environmental taxes in the UK.

5. Options for new green taxes

It is not hard to identify areas of environmental concern in which new or increased taxes could play a role – as part of a broader package including regulation and education. This chapter will consider some of the options for extending environmental taxation, and chapter six will present a specific package of tax reforms for the UK, covering the period 1998–2005.

Energy taxes

The most obvious case is energy use. Energy is the main contributor to a number of environmental problems. Carbon emissions from the burning of fossil fuels to provide industrial, domestic and transport energy are a major cause of the build-up of greenhouse gases in the atmosphere. The world currently emits around 6 gigatonnes (ie. six thousand million tonnes) of carbon from energy generation per year. The World Energy Council has predicted emissions that under a business-as-usual scenario will have risen to around 15 gigatonnes in 2100 (World Energy Council, 1993).

The UK emitted around 148 million tonnes of carbon in 1994 – about 2.5 per cent of the world total. This is on a declining trend (it was 163 million tonnes in 1980). However, this is due primarily to the switch from coal to gas rather than any deliberate environmental policies, as the table shows. (Sectoral figures for 1994 are not yet available). There has been a slight reduction in commercial and public sector emissions, a slight increase in domestic, and a large increase from road transport. The cuts which have been made do not approach the scale of reduction needed if Britain is to play its part in combating global warming. As noted above, the EU has accepted that developed countries will have to make cuts of around 50 per cent.

Table 5.1 UK emissions of carbon dioxide by sector
(million tonnes of carbon)

	1980	1990	1991	1992	1993
Power station	58	54	54	51	46
Domestic	23	22	24	23	24
Commercial/public sector	9	8	9	9	8
Refineries	6	5	5	6	4
Iron and steel	6	7	7	6	6
Other industry	32	25	25	24	24
Road transport	21	30	30	30	30
Other transport	3	4	4	4	4
Other	4	4	3	3	3
Total	**163**	**158**	**159**	**155**	**151**

Global warming is not the only problem associated with energy use. Sulphur and nitrogen dioxide emissions from fossil fuel power stations are the main source of acid rain. Radioactive waste from nuclear power stations poses so-far unanswered questions about safe storage. Wind farms in upland areas can mar precious landscapes. All forms of energy generation have some environmental costs, though some forms are obviously preferable to others. The impact of renewable energy generation pales into insignificance when compared to impact of nuclear power or the burning of fossil fuels. Nevertheless, it remains the case that the "greenest" unit of energy is the unit which is saved rather than used.

UK energy prices have fallen since privatisation, and it is expected that they will fall further as a result of the introduction of competition into energy supply (Corry, Hewett and Tindale, 1996). New energy taxes are needed to ensure that this does not lead to the more wasteful use of energy by British industry.

Options for new energy taxes
Energy taxes can be designed to target specific environmental problems and discourage certain forms of generation. A carbon tax would discourage the burning of fossil fuels, particularly coal. A sulphur tax

would fall most heavily on the use of coal and oil, while a radioactive waste tax would affect only nuclear power. Specific taxes are clearly more flexible, and have the advantage of enabling governments to target environmental issues which they consider to be the most pressing. However, fuel switching may not be desirable. A carbon tax might encourage generators to switch to nuclear power – although the tax rate would have to be fairly high before nuclear power became economically competitive. Although it emits little carbon dioxide, nuclear power generation produces waste which will remain radioactive for many thousands of years, and for which no safe method of management has yet been identified. There are also radioactive emissions and the still-unexplained cancer clusters near nuclear facilities. At one time the industry saw global warming as an argument to be deployed in support of nuclear expansion. But switching from fossil fuels to nuclear would simply mean swapping one set of environmental dangers for another.

Much more likely than a switch to nuclear power would be a further shift from coal to gas. This might seem to be environmentally advantageous. A gas-fired power station produces only half the CO_2 of a coal-fired one, a quarter as much NO_x and no sulphur dioxide (Parker, 1994). The argument that because gas is not as plentiful as coal it should be treated as a "premium fuel" is not a strong one. As a non-renewable resource, gas will run out one day, although new fields continue to be discovered. But this is an argument for a long-term energy policy which develops alternatives to gas which will be ready to replace it when it does run out, not for continuing to burn a dirtier fuel.

The more telling argument against a further "dash for gas" is that using gas is not in fact as clean as it appears. Although carbon dioxide emissions are lower, methane emissions are much higher, particularly because of leakages from the distribution system. And methane is a greenhouse gas, sixty times as powerful molecule for molecule as CO_2. Methane concentrations in the atmosphere have more than doubled since pre-industrial times, and continue to rise rapidly. Methane remains in the atmosphere for only about ten years – a much shorter time than CO_2 – so cuts today would reduce atmospheric concentrations relatively quickly. Tackling methane emissions could therefore be the best way to help mitigate global warming in the short term.

The OECD estimates that if more than 6 per cent of natural gas is lost in distribution, the global warming impact of gas-fired generation will be greater than the impact of burning coal (OECD, 1992). Leakage rates in the

UK are hard to quantify, but could be as high as 11 per cent (Wallis 1991). British Gas Transco claims that they are less than 1 per cent. OFGAS, despite its duty to consider the environmental impact of gas supply, apparently has no opinion on the matter.

A general energy tax would avoid inducements to switch fuel, though there could be exemptions for sectors thought to be in need of encouragement (such as renewables), or some of the revenue could be used to provide direct subsidies for such sectors. A general tax has the great advantage of focusing attention on energy conservation rather than on fuel switching. On balance a general energy tax appears preferable to specific carbon, nitrogen, sulphur or radioactive waste taxes.

Governments also have a range of options on where to levy the tax: on energy production, consumption or an intermediate point. The nearer to the point of production, the fewer points of collection there will be, so there are some administrative arguments in favour of a tax on producers. However, there are two strong arguments in favour of a tax on consumers. First, this would lead to maximum visibility; the tax could be itemised separately on the bill, and there would be no danger of it not being passed on in full to the final consumer (in line with the "polluter pays principle"). Visibility is important in changing behaviour. Second, a tax on producers cannot be levied on non-domestic producers. It might be possible under GATT rules to impose countervailing duties to ensure equal treatment between domestic and non-domestic producers, but this would almost certainly not be permitted under EU rules. So while an EU-wide energy tax might be best imposed on producers, a national one would be better designed as an excise duty on consumers, which would give no advantage to imported energy. It is worth noting that the Finnish energy tax, originally levied on producers, is being transformed into a tax on consumers following Finland's accession to the EU, for precisely this reason.

An end use tax would mean that it would not generally be possible to differentiate between different forms of generation – it would not be possible to exempt, for example, renewable energy delivered through the grid. Companies installing their own renewable generation capacity could be exempted from the tax, which would help develop a decentralised system. (Companies installing their own gas-fired generation, however, should pay the tax). The delivery of energy in the form of heat, from combined heat and power stations, could also be exempted, to encourage this form of energy efficiency. The main support for renewables, however, would have to come from other mechanisms; a revised form of the Non Fossil Fuel Obligation, for example (see Eyre, 1996).

A tax on consumers need not mean a tax on all consumers. For the reasons discussed above, a tax on domestic energy use would be largely ineffective and unacceptably regressive while the housing stock is in such a poor state – although it could be made progressive if introduced at the same time as an eco-bonus or proto-basic income. Failing that, the domestic sector should be excluded from the tax and efficiency in this sector should be promoted through higher building regulations and minimum efficiency standards for domestic appliances.

Excluding the domestic sector would leave around 72 per cent of all UK carbon dioxide emissions (measured by end user) covered by the new energy tax.

Whether or not domestic energy is included, energy taxation should be seen as part of a broader package of measures to promote sustainable energy use. These should include:

● an obligation on all energy suppliers to offer energy services such as advice on management and conservation;

● a clear obligation on energy regulators to promote efficiency;

● support for R&D into clean energy generation, and continuing subsidy to renewable energy generation;

● planning policies which promote the development of renewable energy generation and constrain the development of new fossil-fuel power stations;

● strict regulations on minimum efficiency standards for domestic appliances and buildings.

Revenues from an energy tax would be both secure and substantial, and could therefore be used to make offsetting tax reductions.

Road transport taxes

Transport taxes could be seen as a subset of energy taxes, since transport is a major user of energy. However, there are environmental issues arising from transport patterns which are wider than energy questions, taking in land use, congestion and nature conservation. Moreover, transport taxes are by far the most developed and widely-used form of environmental tax (although not necessarily designed or regarded as such). Transport is therefore worth considering separately.

Over the last 25 years, the average distance travelled per person in Britain each day has risen by almost three quarters. This growth has been made possible by the enormous increase in distance travelled by car – a tenfold increase over the last forty years. In 1989 the Department of Transport predicted that road traffic would increase by between 83 per cent and 142 per cent by 2025, reaching levels which the Government has now conceded would be environmentally unsustainable (the predictions are currently being revised). Transport is a major source of greenhouse gas emissions – 21 per cent of UK carbon emissions are from the transport sector (of which 87 per cent are from road transport). Road transport is also the main cause of urban air pollution, emitting a cocktail of pollutants including nitrogen dioxide, carbon monoxide, particulates and benzene. Air pollution in many European cities can reach dangerous levels when there is insufficient wind to disperse the various gases. The belated introduction of catalytic converters (mandatory on new cars since 1992) is beginning to bring some improvement in air quality, but it is clear that significant increases in traffic volumes would overwhelm this advance.

Table 5.2 Trends in pollution from road transport (1970 emissions = 100)

	1980	1990	1992	1993
Carbon dioxide	133	183	183	188
Carbon monoxide	140	207	200	181
Nitrogen dioxide	136	216	202	187
Black smoke	119	209	217	229
Lead (1975=100)	119	151	147	141

Quite apart from pollution, there are substantial costs arising from accidents and the fear of accidents. Bland official assurances that accident statistics are improving mask the fact that many people are still killed – 3,820 in 1993, or over 10 people per day. 1,250 of these were pedestrians, and 190 cyclists. Society's attitude to those who carelessly destroy others by driving dangerously is reflected in the risibly lenient sentences imposed for motoring sentences by the courts. In addition to the deaths, 44,890 people were seriously injured, and there were over 250,000 other casualties. Moreover, the main reason why accident rates are falling is not that the streets are becoming safer, but that fewer people are using them for walking, cycling or playing in (Hillman and Plowden, 1996).

Finally, there is the cost of congestion. Congestion imposes a heavy burden on industry – the CBI calculates that the annual cost is £15 bn. It also destroys the character and quality of life of many towns and cities. There is now widespread acceptance that it is not possible to build our way out of the problem of congestion, since providing new road space simply encourages further increases in demand. The land-use problem is particularly acute in small, crowded countries such as Britain. We need therefore to move to a policy of trying to control demand for transport. To do this, increased transport taxes are a necessary though not sufficient condition (public investment in alternative transport modes and radical changes in land use planning will also be needed).

There has also been a dramatic increase in freight transport, reaching 212 billion tonne kilometres in 1993. 63 per cent of this went by road. (Royal Commission on Environmental Pollution, 1994). It would obviously be preferable if this went by water or rail, but one should also ask how many of these freight movements could be avoided altogether. The Sustainable Agriculture, Food and Environment (SAFE) Alliance recently documented some of the examples of unnecessary "food miles": fresh milk from a dairy near the south coats of England is sold in the north of Scotland; asparagus on sale in the Vale of Evesham, Britain's main asparagus growing region, is transported by lorry in 2,000 miles from Spain. At present, one British supermarket buys KitKat in France and road freights them to the UK, even though they are also manufactured in Britain. A French retailer buys Mars Bars from Slough, even though they are also made in France. Transport costs are lower than the price differential between the factories. Britain imports 65 per cent of its apples, even though British apples are available most of the year. Apples are imported 14,000 miles from New Zealand, 5,200 miles from South Africa and 3,300 miles from the USA. (In contrast, 90 per cent of the apples sold in France are French.) (Paxton, 1994)

Retailers argue that it is more efficient to operate this way, which may be true in a narrow economic sense, but not in terms of common sense. Increasing freight costs would in any case alter the economic equation. Some environmentalists are suspicious of trade. However, it is not trade *per se* that is the problem, but rather the fact that transport is too cheap. If the price of transport reflected its full social and environmental costs, local produce would become relatively much cheaper. Retailers argue that they import and transport goods to reflect their customers' preference. This is fine, as long as the customers pay a true price. If we want to eat a New Zealand Braeburn, we should pay substantially more for it than we do at the moment.

Options for increasing road transport taxation

The most obvious form of transport tax is fuel duty. In the UK, over two thirds of the cost of a gallon is duty. By European standards, petrol in the UK is relatively cheap: 57p per litre (December 1993) compared to 59p in Germany, 65p in Italy, 66p in France and 67p in the Netherlands. (Royal Commission, 1994). It is also cheaper, in real terms, than it used to be, well below the peak level it reached in 1975. (Johnson, McKay and Smith, 1990). In 1994 the Royal Commission on Environmental Pollution called for a doubling of petrol prices in ten years. As noted above, the Government has recognised the scope for increased fuel duties and introduced the escalator of 5 per cent real increases every year. However, given likely trends in pre-duty prices, which are now predicted to be considerably lower than originally assumed, this will not take prices above their mid-1980s level until 2005. A higher escalator would clearly be justifiable on environmental grounds. The revenue should continue to be treated as part of general government income, making it possible to reduce other taxes.

At present, there is a preferential rate of duty for diesel. This reflects partly economic pressures, since this is the fuel used by the road haulage industry, but partly also a belief that diesel is a "cleaner" fuel than four star petrol. This is now open to considerable doubt. Diesel engines tend to be more fuel efficient, particularly in urban driving conditions, so contribute less to global warming. But in other respects they are highly polluting. Small particulates from diesel engines, known as PM10s, are highly carcinogenic. There is therefore a strong case for taxing diesel at the same rate as four star petrol. Higher diesel charges would increase the cost of distribution, which could feed through into higher consumer prices. But it could also change the balance in favour of more distribution by rail. And it might stop some of the absurdities associated with goods distribution, particularly food, at present.

General fuel taxes are the most straightforward means to internalise the external costs of transport. But there are more specific measures which should also be considered, since they enable governments to target particular issues. For example, 200 lorries travelling only half-full impose a higher environmental burden than 100 full lorries. This could be discouraged through a "capacity-kilometre tax". New Zealand and some states in the US have this form of tax, as did Sweden before its accession to the EU. The Transport Select Committee has recently called for an EU-wide weight and distance tax. The revenue could be used to subsidise rail freight or to develop facilities such as piggy-backing.

One of the most straightforward ways of using the tax system to promote sustainable transport patterns would be to end the absurd treatment of company cars. Tax liability is reduced by one third if the car is driven more than 2,500 miles on business a year, and by two thirds if more than 18,000 miles are driven. A more perverse incentive would be hard to design. In addition, over 900,000 people receive free fuel as a perk from their employers, for which they are undercharged by the Inland Revenue by an average of 25 per cent. This encourages more employees and firms to opt for this perk (Moore and Hanton, 1995).

Vehicle Excise Duty, currently a flat rate of £140 a year for cars, could be reformed to reflect environmental impacts, with lower rates of tax for smaller, less polluting vehicles. The Labour Party is committed to this, and the Government announced at the time of the last Budget that it was looking into it. It could be effective at the margin in encouraging the take-up of less polluting vehicles. It would probably be designed to be revenue neutral – less than £140 for smaller cars, more for larger cars.

A measure which could raise substantial revenue, as well as providing a clear incentive to change behaviour, is a tax on non-domestic private parking. It is estimated that there are three million parking spaces at commercial premises in the UK. Taxing them would target a particularly problematic form of motoring, since it is car-borne commuting which clogs up roads at rush hours and creates pollution peaks. Since travel patterns are fixed, it is also an area where alternative provision can more easily be made. If nobody used a car to commute to work, except perhaps those working shifts which end in the middle of the night, much of the problem would be solved. Business parks and factories, as well as town centres, should be served by public transport, and cycling should be made safer. Employers who encourage their staff to drive to work by offering them free off-street parking should be penalised with a hefty tax.

This tax should not apply to parking spaces at shops, cinemas and the like. These spaces are not private, since they are open to those members of the public using the facilities. And food shopping in particular is an activity for which a car is very useful; however good the public transport, it is not much fun struggling home with several heavy bags and the oranges spilling out all over the bus. Policy makers should seek to control car use, not eliminate it, and thus activities to which a car brings a high marginal value should be relatively untaxed (although a general fuel tax increase will serve to discourage this form of car use along with all others).

However, retailers should not escape altogether. One of the main reasons why people invest in a car is to enable them to shop more easily – and the car is then used for other things as well because the marginal cost of using it is very low. With the advance of cable television and other information technologies, virtual shopping is coming closer. Even before then, telephone shopping could be encouraged. The key is the reintroduction of home deliveries. Any retailer offering off-street parking should be required to offer also home delivery of purchases over a certain value. Some people would then cycle or take public transport to the shop; others could simply phone or fax their order. Those who enjoy visiting supermarkets would then find the car parks less crowded and the aisles less clogged with trolleys. This would be a real extension of consumer choice, surely more valuable than the introduction of yet another brand of catfood.

Revenues from an office parking tax would be secure. They could be used to reduce business rates, as Transport 2000 has suggested (1995). Or they could be used as part of a broader reform programme, to reduce labour taxes.

Motorway tolling

Motorway tolling is common in some countries, including France and Austria. Its suitability for other countries depends very much on geography and the state of the rest of the road network. In small countries with well-developed non-motorway trunk roads, such as the UK, motorway charges could simply displace much of the traffic onto other roads, with considerable disadvantages in terms of safety and the environment. So any tolling would have to be accompanied by measures to make trunk roads less attractive, such as lower speed limits, and even then some diversion would still occur. Alternatively, charges could be restricted to lorries, which could then be banned from using non-motorway routes except where they needed to get from the motorway to the point of collection or delivery. However, this would be complex to administer and open to evasion.

The Government has stated for a number of years that it is considering introducing motorway tolling, most generally in the context of allowing a private company to build a new road and then recoup the cost through tolls. This is what is proposed, for example, for the Birmingham Northern Relief Road. The proposals for motorway tolling have aroused considerable political opposition and the Government can hardly be said to be proceeding with alacrity: in its 1996 White Paper on Transport, some years after the Government had first floated the idea, it had still only got as far as "plans for trials of electronic tolling on motorways".

A scheme to raise money to build more motorways, which this effectively is, is clearly not desirable on environmental grounds. Motorway tolling would be more acceptable as a tool of traffic management. Some diversion of traffic would be inevitable, but using the revenue from motorway tolling directly to subsidise intercity rail transport would mean that the measure might, on balance, have a beneficial effect.

Urban road pricing

Urban road pricing is also on the agenda, but again not making much headway. The Government has sponsored research, and though some of the technical problems are held up as obstacles (despite the successful introduction of road pricing elsewhere in the world), the White Paper states that "the work has confirmed the Government's view that price signals are a highly efficient way of influencing demand for transport". But it has no intention of introducing road pricing itself, and attracting the opprobrium which it is assumed would follow (there is little evidence to support this view, but it is almost universally held). Instead, it plans to "discuss with the Local Authority Associations the case for taking the necessary legislative powers to enable interested local authorities to implement experimental schemes". A more non-committal formulation is hard to imagine. For their part, even the most progressive local authority leaders are wary of introducing road pricing, again because they assume it would cost them votes.

Road pricing is a sub-optimal solution from an environmental perspective, since it is likely to displace some road traffic rather than discouraging road travel altogether. Nevertheless, it may well have a role to play in tackling specific problems, such as urban congestion or local air pollution. Road pricing operated only at certain times could be used to discourage car commuting, leaving most other drivers unaffected.

Road pricing has been effective in reducing demand in Singapore. Work in Cambridge and York suggests that traffic reductions of 15 per cent would be readily achievable. In Central London, according to the Government's Congestion Charging Research Programme, published in 1995, it could reduce traffic by 17 per cent, increase traffic speeds by 26 per cent, reduce accidents by 5 per cent and emissions by 10-20 per cent, and raise £6 billion. However, this would mean a very high charge of £8 per journey into central London.

Those opposed to road pricing sometimes argue that the technology is too complex, and that it could not work in a city the size of London. But it need not be complex; a simple paper disc displayed in the windscreen could work, as it did in Singapore. An electronic system might be the first best option, allowing charges to be calibrated accurately to road use. But a second best, permit-based option would certainly be better than nothing at all. Technological arguments should not be allowed to block progress.

Road pricing is a specific response to particular traffic problems. It should therefore be the responsibility of local government, although in some cases councils will need to act in concert with their neighbours. Central government should make clear that local authorities have the power to introduce road pricing, and use the revenue as they see fit: to increase investment in public transport, to increase other spending or to reduce local taxation. In London, the power should be given to a new city-wide council.

Aviation taxation

Air travel is one of the fastest growing and problematic forms of transport. Between 1974 and 1992 passenger-kilometres travelled on international flights by UK airlines increased by 263 per cent, the number of passengers on international flights using UK airports more than doubled. According to the International Civil Aviation Authority (ICAO), growth in passenger numbers is expected to continue at 5 per cent for at least 20 years. The environmental impacts include noise and land-use issues at ground level, contribution to global warming (through carbon dioxide, NOx and water vapour) and possible contribution to stratospheric ozone destruction. Emissions at high altitude have a significantly greater effect on climate than the equivalent emissions at ground level. In the last twenty years, air transport may have been responsible for up to a quarter of global warming (Barrett 1994). Amelioration measures for one impact typically exacerbate another – quieter planes may be less fuel efficient, for example.

ICAO sets regulations for noise, smoke, carbon monoxide, unburnt hydrocarbons, and nitrogen oxides. However, these are designed to reduce emissions during landing and take-off. There is little consideration given to pollution at altitude. No attempts have been made to regulate for the fuel efficiency of aircraft. ICAO estimates that fuel efficiency of aircraft is increasing at 2-2.5 per cent per year, half the rate of growth in passenger numbers.

ICAO's Chicago Agreement includes a specific exemption from tax for fuel used on international flights. Some have argued that since the exemption is for fuel "in transit", taxing the intake of fuel at a particular airport would be legal. However, this is far from being a universal interpretation of the Chicago Agreement. Moreover, bilateral Air Service Agreements (ASAs) between governments generally include a clause preventing taxation of aviation fuel. This means that none of the externalities associated with air transport are included in the price. Apart from the environmental impacts, this raises issues of fair competition with other transport modes, since road and rail freight do pay fuel taxes on international journeys (though ships do not).

The Royal Commission on Environmental Pollution expresses serious concern about air travel: "an unquestioning attitude towards future growth in air travel, and an acceptance that the projected demand for additional facilities and services must be met, are incompatible with sustainable development". They point to the failure to internalise external costs as the root cause of the problem: "the demand for air transport might not be growing at its present rate if airlines and their customers had to face the costs of the damage they are causing to the environment". They therefore recommend that "the Government negotiate within the EC, and more widely, for the introduction of a levy on fuel purchases by airlines that will reflect the environmental damage caused by aircraft".

Options for new aviation taxes
The best option would be a global aviation fuel tax. The UK government is now calling for this. John Gummer told the Climate Change conference in July 1996 that the UK had "called on ICAO to review the present exemption – and by review, we do not mean look at it and say that nothing can be done".

An alternative approach would be for the EU to redefine flights within its member states as domestic flights, which would get around the Chicago Convention (although it would incur the particular wrath of the Euro-sceptics) and then impose a European aviation fuel tax. There is little danger of diversion: airlines fly to places where people want to go, not to places with the best tax regimes, and extra landings and take-offs consume a vast amount of fuel, so would only be worthwhile if the tax was extremely high. There is a European Directive which prohibits taxing aviation fuel, but this expires in 1997. The difficulty is that bilateral Air Service Agreements would mean that this tax could not be applied to non-EU carriers, even when they were operating on EU-internal flights. This would place EU carriers at a significant disadvantage – unless the key ASAs could be renegotiated.

In the absence of EU action, it would still be possible to tax aviation fuel used on domestic flights within the UK. Short haul flights are more environmentally damaging: energy consumption per passenger is higher since the take-off accounts for more of the total flight. Internal flights are also often unnecessary – or would be if high-speed rail networks were better. Lufthansa has commented that "we are prepared in principle to do without short distance flights. All traffic going for less than two hours should go by rail". (Lufthansa, 1995). Presumably this means two hours flying time. However, ASAs would again mean that a UK tax could not be applied to non-domestic carriers.

Passenger taxes could be used as a blunt tool to increase the cost of air travel, and thus to restrict the increase in passenger miles. But it would not be possible to use this type of tax promote environmental goals more directly, for example by encouraging airlines to invest in less polluting planes. Indeed, the UK Treasury told the Royal Commission explicitly that the recently-introduced tax on air travel – a flat rate charge of £5 per passenger for flights within the EU and £10 for other flights – was not designed to reflect environmental impact.

Alternatively, one could increase airport charges. There would be a slight danger of diversion, particularly from airlines which use London as a clearing house to transfer passengers from long-haul to European flights. But given the current pressure on landing slots, particularly at Heathrow, this is unlikely – and it could be guarded against by a European agreement on minimum airport charges.

Higher airport charges could be used to penalise more polluting aircraft and encourage airlines to invest in more efficient planes by relating the scale of charge to a proxy for emissions, such as weight, engine or airframe. They could also be levied more heavily on short-haul flights. This looks, at present, the most promising option.

Another option would be a noise tax, as recommended by the Royal

Commission. A number of German airport authorities have imposed noise charges on landing aircraft, and some UK airports charge more for noisier planes. It would be effective in addressing the local impact of airports, but not the wider problems: quiet aircraft could be twice as inefficient in fuel use but incur less tax. It should probably only be introduced as part of a broader package of aviation taxes.

Passenger taxes, airport charges or noise taxes could all be imposed on domestic and foreign carriers alike, so would circumvent the difficulties posed by ASAs and the Chicago Convention. The revenues from aviation taxes, whether European or UK, could sensibly be used to modernise and subsidise the high speed rail network.

Waste taxes

A further area where it is possible to use environmental taxes to good effect – and to raise large sums of money – is solid waste. The UK produces around 140 million tonnes of solid waste a year, about three quarters of which arises from industry. About 70 per cent of UK solid waste is currently disposed of in landfill sites. Landfill is generally accepted to be the least desirable environmental option, leading to pollution of surrounding groundwaters and the generation of methane, a greenhouse gas.

UK landfill costs are comparatively low – ranging from £5 to £30 a tonne depending on location (urban costs are higher). Prices are much higher in Italy, France, Germany, and the Netherlands. The cost of landfilling waste is likely to rise substantially in the coming years, due to increasingly strict regulation. Nevertheless, as we have seen, the Government will introduce a tax on landfill disposal of £7 per tonne for most waste, with a lower rate of £2 a tonne for inert waste. The landfill tax is an important and welcome innovation, the first new tax introduced for genuine environmental reasons in the UK. But it is deficient in three respects. First, it is too low, and is unlikely to alter significantly the amount of waste being sent to landfill. The Government should have announced that the £7 rate was a first instalment, and that there would be annual increases until the tax had a more substantial incentive effect. This would have sent a clear signal to waste producers, without inducing a sudden jump in their costs. The Danish landfill tax started at £4.50 a tonne, and will have increased to £33 per tonne by 1997.

Second, it makes a distinction between inert and "active" waste (ie waste which decays and will give off methane and has the potential to pollute groundwater or contaminate soil), but not between active waste and hazardous waste. The latter obviously has greater potential to pollute. The Labour Party has proposed a third and higher band for hazardous waste. Landfill operators already distinguish between hazardous and non-hazardous waste (and charge more for the former), so a new rate would not be difficult to administer, though there would no doubt be extensive lobbying by companies producing waste on the borderline.

Third, the tax applies only to landfilled waste, and not to all waste disposal. Most commentators agree that there is a hierarchy of waste management options: minimisation; re-use; recycling; incineration; landfill. To the extent that the new tax alters behaviour, it will push waste up the hierarchy to incineration. But the main environmental benefits come from minimisation, re-use and recycling. (Indeed Greenpeace argues that incineration is actually worse than landfilling, because it leads to an increase in emissions of toxic dioxins.) The tax should therefore logically be applied to all waste disposal. Again this is the approach used in Denmark, although incineration attracts a lower rate (£23 a tonne).

Should the tax apply to incinerators which generate electricty? There is a complex set of issues surrounding the role of waste-to-energy plants in sustainable waste management and a sustainable energy policy. Some argue that waste-to-energy plants, particularly large ones which need a big supply of waste to operate economically, encourage waste creation and undercut re-use and recycling. There are also pollution problems associated with even the cleanest incinerator. Others argue that however efficiently waste is avoided, re-used or recycled, there will always be some in need of disposal, and that incineration is the best option for this. Moreover, if waste-to-energy plants displace generation from older fossil-fuel plants the net impact on pollution could well be positive. On balance we favour the latter view.

By the end of 1996 all municipal waste incineration in the UK (which accounts for around 80 per cent of the solid waste incinerated) will incorporate energy recovery. It would be possible to exempt this from the tax, leaving only clinical and hazardous waste incineration liable for the tax (and there is considerable scope for waste reduction in both sectors). Or it would be possible to introduce another tax band for incineration plus energy recovery, as the Danes do (this would mean potentially five tax bands in the waste disposal tax: landfill of hazardous waste; landfill of active waste; landfill of inert waste; incineration; incineration plus energy recovery). The best option of all might be to exempt only the most thermally-efficient energy recovery plants, those with combined heat and power capacity. These will be tend to be smaller plants, so avoid the concerns about large incinerators undercutting the market for recycling. Waste to energy plants without CHP capacity would then pay the same tax rate as incinerators without energy recovery.

One of the difficulties with waste taxation is that for domestic waste, households do not pay on the basis of volume produced, so have little incentive to reduce (the extent of this problem should not be exaggerated, since household waste accounts for only 5 per cent of the total). In Denmark, the waste disposal tax is identified separately on council tax bills, which at least brings the message to the attention of the public. Some municipalities in the USA and Ireland have experimented with schemes which charge households on a per-bag or per-dustbin basis. Supporters of such schemes argue that they have worked well, and that the feared increase in fly-tipping and stuffing of neighbours' dustbins has not occurred (Repetto, 1992) Those involved in waste management in the UK tend to be sceptical about the feasibility of such as approach here; perhaps the residents of Camden and Cambridge have less sense of responsibility than those in Washington State or Wexford. But there is no reason why a local authority wishing to try this approach should not be allowed to do so. One of the advantages of a less centralised system than the UK is that it allows for experimentation and innovation: this is as true for environmental policies as for any other area.

Local authorities could be given powers to levy taxes on particular products, for example disposable plates, cups or packaging from take-away food. This would be appropriate, as it is they who have to deal with the waste and often with the litter. Allowing local authorities to experiment would be the best means of identifying the optimum forms of taxation.

As with energy and transport, taxation alone will not deliver sustainable waste management. The package of measures introduced alongside the tax should include:

● encouragement to local authorities and others to develop recycling services, particularly for products such as aluminium cans where the environmental gains of recycling are high and public awareness relatively low;

● regulations on the minimum recycled content of newspapers and other goods, to boost demand for recycled materials;

- planning policies which constrain the availability of waste disposal options;

- the phasing out of substances such as PVC which are particularly hazardous to the environment whatever waste management option is used, and those which are particularly problematic for incineration;

The revenue stream from waste taxes will be secure, so the money should be part of the general Exchequer.

A quarrying tax

The proverbially useless job-creation scheme is one in which some people dig holes in the ground and others come along and fill them in again. This is being done every day, on a macro-scale, with the quarrying and waste disposal industries (often the same companies operate in both sectors). Aggregates companies create the holes by extracting rock, sand and gravel, which they then sell very cheaply. Because primary aggregates are so cheap, there is little demand for recycled ones. So demolition waste – rock, sand, gravel – is mostly sent to landfills, to fill in the holes. During this pointless cycle, some people get very rich, and many more suffer serious disamenity. There is damage to landscapes, often in beauty spots, resulting from quarrying. According to the CPRE "an area three times the size of the Isle of Wight is currently under mineral working – this is expected to double at current rates of expansion". Footpaths and public access are lost. Traffic is generated, often in previously-quiet areas, and there is lots of noise and dust for nearby residents. Quarrying can also result in a loss of aquifer capacity, with consequent reduction in water supply, and surface water pollution.

The construction industry needs a reliable supply of aggregates. But there is a plentiful supply of secondary aggregates which could reduce – though not eliminate – the need for new quarrying. Annual demand in the UK is currently running at around 300 million tonnes a year of primary aggregates; this is predicted to grow to 400 million by 2011 (DoE, 1992). There is 70 million tonnes of construction and demolition waste every year. Little of this is re-used, partly because landfilling for construction waste is very cheap and partly because the market price for primary aggregates is so low.

A package of measures to reduce quarrying and increase the use of secondary aggregates would need to include a quarrying tax to make primary aggregates more expensive, a landfill tax to make the disposal of construction waste more expensive, planning restrictions on new quarries, particularly such environmental monstrosities as the coastal "superquarries" planned for Scotland, and changed specifications, especially for roads, to make use of secondary aggregates easier. An end to widespread road-building, which would be part of any move to a more sustainable economy, would also reduce demand for primary aggregates.

Even with all these measures in place, it is unlikely that the demand for primary aggregates would be very responsive to price. The consultancy ECOTEC predicted that a 50 per cent tax would reduce demand by 16 per cent, and a 100 per cent tax by 30 per cent (ECOTEC, 1991). There is therefore scope to raise a lot of money, which should be seen as part of the general Exchequer.

Air and water pollution charges

Since the 1989 Water Act, a system of discharge "consents" has been operated by the NRA/Environment Agency. Companies pay for the right to discharge pollutants to water or to the air. HMIP operated a similar system with regard to IPC. However, the fees are set on a cost-recovery basis and are not directly related to the volume of pollution. They cannot therefore be described as green taxes, although they could relatively easily be converted into taxes (Smith, 1995). This would give companies a greater incentive to reduce pollution than regulation alone.

Agricultural input charges

One aspect of water pollution where it is difficult to charge specific discharges is pollution from farms. The run-off from fields cannot be measured in the way that discharges from factory pipes can be. It is therefore easier to tax inputs via an excise duty on fertilisers and pesticides. This would not only improve the water environment, it would also help provide a "level growing field" so that cleaner, organic farming became more economically competitive.

It is not clear how much taxes on pesticides or fertilisers would reduce use. It might be the case that they would simply raise revenue, which could be used to help clean up the water environment. It might even become possible to reduce domestic customers' bills. Significant changes in behaviour will have to await the demise of the Common Agricultural Policy in its present form – an event brought nearer by the need to expand the EU to Eastern Europe.

6. A Reform package for the UK – 1997-2005

Would environmental tax reform be progressive or regressive? Would it lead to higher employment, and if so how much? Would it damage or enhance the competitiveness of British industry? And how much would it benefit the environment?

The answer to these and most other questions on the subject depends on which particular environmental taxes are involved, how they are implemented and what the revenues are used for. The debate cannot be advanced very far at the abstract level. IPPR therefore commissioned Cambridge Econometrics to model a package of different measures for the period 1997-2005.

The Cambridge E3 model for the UK

The Cambridge Multisectoral Dynamic Model is a large-scale integrated model of the UK economy and its regions, which has been extended to include energy-environment-economy interactions (becoming an "E3" model).

The energy sub-model allows a detailed analysis of the demand for energy and the substitution between fuels following the imposition of an energy tax.

The model is comparatively simple in structure. It has some 26 equations for economic and energy variables estimated by co-integration techniques, which allows the long-term solution to be distinguished from short-term dynamics. But despite this simplicity, its variables are highly disaggregated: it distinguishes 49 industries, 38 investment sectors, 10 fuels, 10 air emissions and 12 regions.

The taxes

Cambridge Econometrics modelled a package of seven new or increased environmental taxes and two scenarios for recycling the revenues to preserve fiscal neutrality (ie. with the PSBR remaining as it was in the base case).

1. A commercial and industrial energy tax

The aim of this tax is to encourage the efficient use of energy. This is applied to all forms of energy at the point of end use, excluding household energy consumption to avoid regressive impact, and also fuel inputs to electricity generation to avoid double taxation (since the electricity is taxed). An energy tax was chosen in preference to a carbon tax to focus attention on conservation and avoid further incentives to fuel switching from coal to gas or nuclear. An end use tax was chosen to ensure equal treatment between indigenous energy and imported energy such as that from the electricity interconnector with France. The tax starts at $1 per barrel of oil equivalent in 1997 and increased $1 a year to $9 per barrel in 2005. This is similar to the level envisaged in the EU's carbon/energy tax proposal.

The tax raises just under £1 billion in the first year, £2 billion in the second year, £3 billion in 1999 and £10.5 billion in 2005.

2. An increased landfill tax

The aim here is to strengthen the incentive to minimise waste production. The tax is increased by £2 per tonne per year, from £7 per tonne in 1997 (the rate proposed by the current Government) to £25 per tonne in 2005. As a comparison, Denmark's landfill tax is currently £33 per tonne. The lower rate, for inert wastes, is also increased by £2 a year, from £2 to £18. Although such wastes do less environmental damage, a tax is needed to encourage the recycling of demolition waste and thus avoid quarrying. In Denmark, where there is no lower rate, recycling of demolition wastes has increased from 12 per cent to 82 per cent since the introduction of the landfill tax.

The revenue is £700 million in the first year, rising to £2.7 billion in 2005.

3. A higher road fuel escalator

The aim here is to bring about a rise in the real price of road fuel. As noted above, the 5 per cent escalator will leave prices in 2005 the same in real terms as they were in the mid-1970s and mid-1980s (assuming predicted oil price trends are accurate). We therefore propose an 8 per cent a year real increase in fuel duty from 1997. In addition, diesel duty would increase to the same as duty on leaded petrol in 1997: recent evidence on the health impacts of diesel fumes means that there is no justification for treating diesel as a cleaner fuel or encouraging its use.

The increase in the escalator raises an extra £450 million in 1997, rising to £6.8 billion in 2005.

4. A quarrying tax

To strengthen the incentive to recycle demolition waste, a tax to increase the price of virgin aggregates is needed. A tax of £1 per tonne is imposed in 1997, rising £1 a year to £9 per tonne in 2005. Similar taxes exist in Denmark and the Netherlands.

Revenues are £223 million in the first year, rising to £2.4 billion in 2005.

5. An office parking tax

This is to discourage car commuting, and would be levied on all parking spaces at workplaces. It would not be levied on parking spaces used by the public – for example at leisure facilities or shops. The tax would be introduced at £1 per week per space in 1997, rising to £8 per week in 2005. It is estimated that there are 3 million office parking spaces. There is little evidence available on the price elasticity of demand for office parking spaces. An annual charge of £52 per space would probably not be enough to induce significant changes in behaviour, but a charge of £416 per year probably would. Since the rates will be announced in advance, we have assumed a steady annual reduction of 5 per cent a year.

6. An end to company car perks

This is not a new tax or a tax increase, but the removal of an existing distortion. It should be done, and we therefore build it into the model assumptions. Mileage banding is ended, and the provision of free fuel is taxed at a proper rate. Revenue is £480 million in the first year, falling to £350 million in 2005.

Table 6.1 Revenues from new taxes

Tax (£ bn)	1997	1998	1999	2000	2005
Energy	1.3	2.5	3.7	4.8	8.8
Landfill	0.557	0.736	0.905	1.1	1.9
Road fuel	0.506	1.1	1.7	2.4	8
Quarrying	0.205	0.404	0.608	0.837	2.1
Office parking	0.095	0.179	0.244	0.300	0.520
Company cars	0.481	0.425	0.387	0.367	0.349
Total	3.1	4.2	7.5	9.8	21.7

Scenarios for recycling the revenues

The economist's package

In this scenario all of the revenue is used to reduce employers' NICs. This is the strategy likely to result in the largest overall increase in employment. Other modelling suggests that the largest increase in jobs would come from targeted reductions at the lower end of the scale, facilitating the creation of jobs for the unskilled (see appendix 2), but it was not possible to simulate this in the MDM model.

The rate of Employer's National Insurance Contribution is reduced by 1.3 percentage points in 1997, 2.26 per cent in 1998, 3.2 per cent in 1999, 4 per cent in 2000 and 6.9 per cent in 2005.

The politician's package

This scenario recognises that some of the revenue will be needed to win the support of particular groups in society for the reforms:

● To appeal to the public and offset some of the increased cost of motoring, the standard rate of VAT is cut by 0.2 percentage points in 1997, 0.4 per cent in 1998, 0.6 per cent in 1999, 0.8 per cent in 2000, and 1.7 per cent in 2005.

● In recognition of the fact that small businesses are less able to react to tax changes by altering behaviour, some of the revenue is used to reduce business rates by 3 percentage points.

● The rest is used to reduce employers' NICs, by 1 per cent in 1997, 1.7 per cent in 1998, 2.3 per cent in 1999, 2.9 per cent in 2000 and 4.5 per cent in 2005.

Environmental effects

The reform delivers substantial reductions in emissions of key pollutants. In particular, it delivers a reduction of 9 per cent, compared to the base scenario, in total UK carbon emissions in 2005. The main reductions are from road transport (19 per cent), iron and steel (18 per cent), chemicals (12 per cent) and other industry (10 per cent). The reform also produces a 6 per cent reduction in sulphur dioxide emissions, with the largest reduction (19 per cent) coming from road transport.

There is also a substantial reduction in the amount of waste produced. Total waste disposal falls by 6 per cent in 2000 and 16 per cent in 2005. Landfill is reduced by 18 per cent in 2005.

Table 6.2 Reductions in carbon emissions by fuel
(thousand tonnes of carbon)

	1997	1998	1999	2000	2005
Coal and coke	287	946	1562	2158	4966
Motor spirit	98	284	555	897	2853
Derv	62	178	348	562	1788
Gas oil	64	119	171	221	391
Fuel oil	27	28	104	191	377
Other refined oil	61	111	163	211	409
Gas	236	501	728	943	1881
Total	781	2166	3631	5185	12665

Table 6.3 Reductions in carbon dioxide emissions by sector
(thousand tonnes of CO_2)

	1997	1998	1999	2000	2005
Power generation	0	442	843	1257	3423
Own use of energy	38	100	162	224	437
Iron and steel	190	366	527	676	1140
Mineral production	10	22	35	50	133
Chemicals	110	175	245	298	455
Other industry	131	283	451	624	1377
Rail transport	3	6	8	11	20
Road transport	160	462	903	1460	4641
Water transport	2	6	11	15	31
Air transport	7	14	20	25	47
Domestic final use	76	187	276	355	664
Other final use	55	104	151	191	296
Total	781	2166	3631	5185	12665

Table 6.4 Reductions in carbon dioxide emissions by sector
(per cent)

	1997	1998	1999	2000	2005
Power generation	0	1.11	2.17	3.24	7.87
Own use of energy	0.38	0.98	1.57	2.15	4.16
Iron and steel	2.48	4.85	7.03	8.99	17.36
Mineral production	0.37	0.78	1.27	1.82	5.29
Chemicals	2.13	3.48	4.97	6.18	11.08
Other industry	0.87	1.89	3.03	4.23	10.12
Rail transport	0.60	1.19	1.77	2.32	4.47
Road transport	0.53	1.55	3.06	5.02	18.84
Water transport	0.14	0.38	0.65	0.90	1.77
Air transport	0.83	1.57	2.21	2.79	4.70
Domestic final use	0.33	0.80	1.17	1.50	2.71
Other final use	0.79	1.54	2.29	2.98	5.30
Total	0.54	1.51	2.56	3.67	9.14

Economic effects

Under the Economist's package, there are 252,000 extra jobs in 2000, and 717,000 in 2005. Unemployment falls by 300,000; this difference is because not all those who fill the new jobs are registered as unemployed. GDP is virtually unchanged – up 0.31 per cent in 2000, down 0.03 per cent in 2005 – both infinitesimal in relation to error margins. There is an increase in inflation of less than 0.25 per cent a year, insignificant in relation to model error. The balance of payments deteriorates very slightly, owing to the relative price effects. On balance the change in relative prices diverts activity from sectors whose output is traded to sectors whose output is traded less or not at all. The total deterioration of the current account is barely half a percent of GDP – again not statistically significant.

Owing to the more labour intensive production, the share of wages in GDP rises slightly. Profits are a residual in the model so are particularly sensitive to small changes in the projections. With that caveat, it seems that profits rise compared to baseline in nominal terms but slightly more slowly than nominal GDP. They grow slightly more slowly than retail prices so are constant or slightly down in real terms. Once again, the differences are small compared to model error. Qualitatively speaking, there is no large change in profits and they certainly do not fall sharply as a consequence of the switch. Fears of capital flight would appear therefore to be unfounded. (Of course, the variation across sectors is more important than the aggregate movement.)

Table 6.5 Economist's Package: differences in macro variables – difference from base scenario
(PSBR held constant)

	1997	1998	1999	2000	2005
GDP at constant prices (1990)	£487m	£1,016m	£1,502m	£1,773m	-£207m
	0.09%	0.19%	0.27%	0.31%	-0.03%
Employment	40,000	99,000	171,000	253,000	717,000
	0.16%	0.38%	0.65%	0.95%	2.56%
RPI (1990=100)	-0.18	-0.2	-0.02	0.44	6.43
	-0.12%	-0.12%	-0.01%	0.25%	3.06%

The Politician's Package

This is inferior in job creation terms: it produces 576,000 new jobs rather than 717,000. The impact on GDP, the balance of payments and the RPI remains marginal (with the cut in VAT making the inflation impact even more negligible than in the Economist's Package).

Table 6.6 Politician's Package: differences in macro variables – difference from base scenario
(PSBR held constant)

	1997	1998	1999	2000	2005
GDP at constant prices (1990)	£457m	£957m	£1,363m	£1,524m	£1775m
	0.09%	0.18%	0.24%	0.26%	-0.27%
Employment	32,000	80,000	139,000	206,000	576,000
	0.12%	0.31%	0.53%	0.78%	2.06%
RPI (1990=100)	-0.33	-0.47	-0.39	-0.04	5.68
	-0.21%	-0.29%	-0.23%	-0.02%	2.70%

Despite its macro-economic inferiority, the politician's package is more likely to be accepted and implemented. The rest of this chapter therefore concentrates on the modelling results for that scenario. The trends, in terms of type of employment, sectoral and regional distribution, are in any case similar between the two scenarios.

Table 6.7 Differences in employment by employment type – thousands
(politician's package)

	1997	1998	1999	2000	2005
Full time	20.5	49.1	83.9	122.8	325.7
Part time	7.4	19.5	35.3	54.7	177.3
Self-employed	4.4	11.2	19.5	28.7	73.3
Total	32.3	79.8	138.7	206.2	576.3

Table 6.8 Differences in employment by region – thousands
(politician's package)

	1997	1998	1999	2000	2005
Greater London	4.6	12.1	21.3	32.0	89.5
Rest of South East	6.2	16.4	29.4	44.7	131.0
East Anglia	1.6	3.6	6.0	8.6	21.3
South West	1.7	4.4	7.9	12.0	35.9
West Midlands	3.1	7.3	12.4	18.3	52.5
East Midlands	2.4	5.5	9.4	13.9	35.0
Yorkshire and Humberside	2.7	6.6	11.3	16.4	43.1
North West	3.2	8.3	14.3	21.1	59.3
North	2	4.5	7.5	10.9	29.9
Wales	1.4	3.6	6.3	9.5	26.5
Scotland	2.6	5.9	10.2	15.1	43.3
Northern Ireland	0.7	1.7	2.7	3.8	8.9
Total	32.2	79.7	138.7	206.3	576.4

Sectoral employment

The most significant increases are in health and social work (126,000), business services (69,500), education (51,500) and construction (40,000), but employment in manufacturing industry is also simulated to increase.

Table 6.9 Differences in employment by sector – thousands
(politician's package)

	1997	1998	1999	2000	2005
Agriculture	0.4	1.1	2.0	2.9	8.6
Manufacturing	9.0	19.6	31.6	44.7	112.2
Utilities	0.3	0.7	1.4	2.3	6.7
Construction	3.1	7.7	13.2	18.8	40.6
Distribution, hotels	4.3	11.1	19.9	29.4	68.0
Transport and communications	1.4	3.4	5.7	8.0	17.7
Other market services	6.1	17.1	31.9	48.3	119.6
Non-market services	7.5	18.9	32.9	51.8	203.0
Total	32.2	79.7	138.7	206.3	576.4

Are the modelling results credible?

Economic modelling is necessarily an inexact science. These simulations are, moreover, taking many variables outside the range of historical observation, when predictions become unusually hazardous. The results should not, therefore, be taken as a quantitatively-reliable guide to what will happen. What matters is the broad tendencies which they reveal – negligible impact on GDP and inflation, a significant increase in employment – rather than the precise figures.

The employment gains seem very large to the intuition of many, but it should be remembered that they are not immediate. The average annual increase in employment is some 70,000 or about a quarter of one percent of the labour force. Moreover, these results reveal similar trends to studies of environmental tax reform carried out elsewhere in Europe. For example, the Deutsches Institut fur Wirtschaftung predicted an increase in employment of 600,000 after 10 years, and insignificant impacts on economic growth and competitiveness. Estimated energy use declined by 7 per cent. The European Commission paper *Taxation, Social Security Systems and the Environment* suggests that after 7 years, both employment and GDP would be up by 1 per cent. This study also looked at the impact of targeting the cuts in employers' contributions to the low paid. This leads to more positive employment benefits: employment rises by 2.2 per cent rather than 1 per cent (European Commission, 1993a).

The impact on households – is the package regressive?

Any increase in employment will be a significant contribution to social justice, since unemployment is the main cause of poverty in the UK today. But what about the impact on low-income households who do not see their income rise due to increased employment? They will benefit from the environmental improvement; often disproportionately so. But will they be better or worse off in financial terms?

The only tax change which bears directly on households is higher petrol duty. In general, motoring taxes are progressive. There will be groups particularly hard hit; notably those who live in rural areas inadequately served by public transport. It was not possible, in the Cambridge Econometrics model, to target our tax reductions on particular groups, but one option would be to increase Revenue Support Grant to rural councils, allowing them to levy lower Council Taxes.

The other tax changes might feed through to consumer in the form of higher prices, though reductions in labour taxes will leave many producers unaffected or better off. The overall impact on the RPI, as we have seen, is negligible. But do the poor buy more of the energy-intensive goods which might increase in price? The main items in low-income household budgets are housing, food, fuel, clothing and household goods (Bradshaw, 1993). Of these, housing costs and fuel would be unaffected; food, clothing and household goods would be made cheaper. In addition, in the Politician's Package, a 1.5 per cent in the rate of VAT would benefit all households, though not by very much.

7. Conclusion: A green tax commission

A British government should undertake a radical reform of the tax system in order to introduce new market mechanisms to protect the environment and cut distortionary taxation. However, as we have argued, the way in which the reform is carried out is crucial. The package has to be well designed if it to have a substantial impact on environmental quality, avoid hurting the poor, help rather than hinder British business. Despite the urgency of the environmental imperative, therefore, the ground for tax reform should be carefully prepared.

Many countries have established environmental tax commissions to consider the scope for reform and recommend the best package. In 1994 Canada's Minister of the Environment and Minister of Finance jointly convened a task force of tax experts from the government, industry and environmental groups, to investigate the scope for environmental tax reform. The Netherlands established a Commission in March 1995. Also in 1995, Sweden established a Parliamentary Commission, consisting of twelve members of parliament and a number of experts, to consider further greening of the Swedish tax system. Norway and Belgium also have Green Tax Commission, and Austria has a carbon dioxide commission. We believe that it would be sensible to establish a Green Tax Commission for the UK.

Composition

The Commission's membership should be broadly based. Since the aim is not only to design a good package, but also to build maximum support for it, there would be little point excluding groups likely to be hostile. Having said that, this is a complex area in which every industrial sector and almost every type of pubic interest group, will perceive a direct interest and seek representation. So a strict limit should be set on numbers – probably no more than twenty or twenty five people in total.

The views of the manufacturing sector, the services sector and the small business sector should all be represented, as should the perspective of the emerging environmental industries sector. Trade unions, environmental groups, consumer organisations and local authorities should participate.

From within Government, there should be representatives from the Treasury, Customs and Excise, the Inland Revenue, the DoE, the DTI, the Department of Transport (if it still exists) and the Environment Agency. Some independent tax experts and economists should also be included.

To underline its official standing, the Commission should be serviced from within the Treasury, and should be chaired by the Chancellor of the Exchequer.

Timetable

Harold Wilson's withering remark about Royal Commissions ("Take minutes, last years") must not be allowed to become applicable to the Green Tax Commission. The Commission should be given a firm timetable. Suppose the Commission is created in May or June 1997, immediately after a General Election (It is probably too much to hope for any movement before then, given the nervousness from all sides about letting the electorate into a sensible debate about taxation.) It could be told to produce its report the following May or June. The Chancellor could then announce the Government's response in November. More straightforward reforms could be enacted at once, but the more complex measures could usefully be handled in the way that the landfill tax was, with a period for genuine consultation between the announcement and the enacting legislation.

Terms of reference

The problem with in-depth consideration and consultation is that it opens the door to all sorts of special pleading and misrepresentation. Vested interests will deploy all their powers of obfuscation – which are considerable – both to block progress on the Commission and to frighten the Government during the consultation. A thousand objections will be raised: some of them jejune theorising on issues which have been covered many times before, others technical questions on issues so minor as to be barely worthy of response. Those who oppose change will join with those hoping for lucrative consultancy contracts in pressing for more research. A sustained attempt will be made to drown out the Commission's voice in elegantly-phrased yelps of self-interest.

But we should remember John Gummer's stricture – "the time for looking is past". We have had, on global warming, a decade of co-ordinated international research. In the UK, it is seven years since the publication of *Blueprint for a Green Economy* sparked off the debate about using market mechanisms in environmental policy; six years since the Government's White Paper *This Common Inheritance* proposed the wider use of fiscal measures. The fossil fuel lobby has spent those years supporting environmental taxes "in principle" while opposing them in practice. Taxes in principle are no good – no one pays them.

We believe that the case for green tax reform is sufficiently strong for a Government to announce that it is setting up a Commission to consider not whether to proceed, but how to proceed. It should announce a target, expressed as a certain percentage of its total revenue or as a percentage of GDP, of taxes to be shifted off labour and onto pollution and waste. The aim would be for the Commission to draw up proposals for an eight-year programme of reform, along the lines of the one proposed here. When the Government announces its proposals, it should be made clear that the consultation is also about how to implement its plans, not about whether to proceed at all. Again the landfill tax offers a model: the Government was prepared to drop its proposals for an *ad valorem* tax, accepting the view from industry and others that a weight based tax would be preferable. It was not prepared to listen to those arguing against any tax at all.

The taxes we propose here would bring in over £20 billion a year once fully phased in. This represents roughly 3 per cent of GDP or 10 per cent of current government revenues. Since there are many others taxes which we considered but did not model, this would be an achievable and realistic target. To avoid long disputes about exactly which current taxes constitute "environmental" ones, any taxes in effect before the creation of the Commission should be excluded from the 10 per cent figure. The Green Tax Commission should therefore be given the following terms of reference:

> To consider ways in which the Government can meet its target of raising a further 10 per cent of its revenues from taxes on resource use, pollution and waste within a decade (with corresponding reductions in other taxes), and to make recommendations within one year.

Changes at European level would be preferable, reducing transitional difficulties and potential impacts on competitiveness. But while taxation remains the preserve of member states – and this will remain the case for the foreseeable future – concerted action will be very difficult. Action must therefore be taken on a unilateral basis; our results indicate that it is possible to act alone and still achieve improvements in environmental quality and increases in employment.

In the absence of action, environmental decline will manifest itself in public health effects that not even the most myopic of politicians can ignore. The social fabric cannot survive with existing levels of unemployment. Bold and imaginative measures are essential. The restructuring of the tax system on the lines suggested here would be a fitting project for any government, but should appeal particularly to a radical and progressive one.

Appendix I
Indirect taxation is not as bad as you think
Dan Corry
Senior Economist, IPPR

The Problems with Direct Tax

In the last election, Labour went to the country on policies for tax that would have left – as independent experts confirmed – 8 out of 10 families better off and a further 1 out of 10 no worse off. But Labour lost.

A policy of increasing direct taxes, even where the money is used exclusively to reduce it for others, appears to lead to enormous problems in the political market place, particularly for Labour. It worries people trying to manage the household budget, who imagine it will hit them wherever the actual cut-off is; it has become associated with putting a cap on aspirations, since everyone wants to be rich; the redistribution it represents seems to many to be an attack on hard workers and achievers in favour of lazy good-for-nothings; and higher taxes on the rich are too easily given a gloss as the politics of envy.

There is a hope that given the substantial tax increases imposed since 1992, the stigma against direct tax increases will have gone, or at least have been neutralised. But while there has undoubtedly been a partial shift, the assumption of a total conversion of the public's antipathy to direct tax seems highly dodgy, particularly since the government has taken great care to avoid any increase in marginal tax rates.

Intellectually too, there are points that suggest direct tax should be down-played as the major source of revenue and redistribution. Evasion and avoidance are much easier than in expenditure based systems, while international globalisation makes it harder to have income tax rates way out of line with competitor countries.

What then should the progressive policy maker do? Give up on the idea of taxation to raise revenue and redistribute income? If we lean less on direct tax, how are we to raise money for public services?

There are some things that could be done within the tax system that sidestep the direct/indirect issue. Recent trends in inequality seem to have something to do with unearned income, inheritance and self-employment income, and these may be sensible areas to look at again – if the policies can be presented as not being anti-saving or against "enterprise".

But the "easy" things are few and we will have to tackle traditionally difficult areas. It may well be that we must look at indirect taxes to raise money.

Indirect taxes

My contention – and it is certainly not unchallengeable – is that the public may be happier to pay indirect taxes than direct ones. The example of VAT on fuel shows that this is no foregone conclusion – although I believe that salience of the 8 per cent VAT on fuel has fallen away relatively fast. However, increases in other indirect taxes recently, including the introduction of new taxes on things like insurance and holiday flights and the 5 per cent fuel tax escalator, have not provoked much opposition.

The public are not strongly against indirect tax mainly because it is less obviously a deduction from their basic pay. However daft, they feel that expenditure taxes have a choice element: one does not have to buy the taxed item. It is not so obviously the government taking money off you – indeed most of the money is paid over to shopkeepers not to the evil taxman. And this is not to mention the fact that if people can be convinced that the tax influences behaviour in a way they generally approve off (eg tobacco and green taxes) then they feel less hostility to them. Direct taxes by contrast are seen – wrongly – to affect work incentives.

But just because the punters think more kindly of them does not mean we should start going down this road, if we really feel they inevitably open up inequality. My argument is that they do not do this as much as one thinks. While it is hard to argue that in themselves indirect taxes are more progressive than sensibly designed and enforced direct ones, this is insufficient to dismiss them as progressive policy options.

How regressive are indirect taxes?

The degree of regressiveness of indirect taxes depends very much on the structure of such taxes. To take some examples:

● exemptions can make them more progressive (eg exempting food from VAT)

- differential rates can help by, for instance, making items that feature more in the budgets of richer people subject to higher rates of indirect tax.

- "free" allowances can be given, so that maybe each person had a VAT-free allowance of fuel.

What this illustrates is that just as one can have a more or less progressive income tax system, so too one can vary the degree of progressivity of indirect tax by appropriate design. The call might be for better designed indirect tax systems rather than for a boycotting of them altogether.

Offsetting the effects of indirect taxes on the poorer groups
But we must not only look at the initial incidence of such taxes We must look at the overall effect they have on inequality, setting the regressive revenue raising aspects alongside the progressive effects of the things that the revenue buys. This happens in two ways.

First, some of the revenue raised can be used to offset at least some of the regressive impacts. The Institute of Fiscal Studies has shown, for instance, how one can have a carbon tax, offset the effects on low income families and still have a lot of money to spend on services that improve the quality of life, especially for the lower income groups.

This is not to deny problems of targeting or the traps that means tested benefits can give. Indeed it may be better to make some progressive income tax cuts with the money than to rely on the social security system.

Using the money from indirect taxes for benefits in kind
The second way we can use the money is to provide things that are disproportionately useful and used by poorer households (at least disproportionately in relation to their income).

The Table overleaf gives a very important perspective on this, showing the different impact of taxes and benefits on income distribution. Comparing columns 2 and 3 one sees that cash benefits have a very big impact on equalling up what begins as an extraordinarily unequal distribution.

Direct tax does make a further contribution to evening up the distribution, as one would expect. There are two points to make on this. First, the impact on the ratio of the top to bottom 10 per cent is in fact rather limited. Secondly it does appear, on these figures, that the direct tax system has become more progressive in some respects in recent years. Figures for 1990 (Economic Trends January 1993) show that direct tax only shifted the top 20 per cent to bottom 20 per cent ratio from 14.2 per cent to 15.3 per cent.

Indirect tax (as we can see from comparing columns 4 and 5) is – as expected – regressive in its impact, eliminating the progressive effects of direct tax.

Table AI.1 The importance of benefits in kind in redistribution
(Annual household income in 1993)

		+cash benefits	-direct tax	-indirect tax	+benefits in kind
		=	=	=	=
	Original Income	Gross Income	Disposable Income	Post tax Income	Final Income
Bottom 20%	£1920	£6380	£5590	£3870	£7480
Bottom 10%	£1471	£5639	£4825	£3036	£7055
Top 20%	£39370	£40420	£31100	£26200	£28270
Top 10%	£48754	£49665	£38003	£32614	£34456
Bottom 20% as %age of top 20%	4.9%	15.8%	18.0%	14.8%	26.5%
Bottom 10% as %age of top 10%	3.0%	11.4%	12.7%	9.3%	20.5%

(Source: Economic Trends, December 1994, Tables B and 3A (Appendix 1)
Figures refer to all households, ranked by equivalised income

The thing to focus on most however is the impact of benefits in kind on distribution. This reflects the key importance of free, universally available public service like health, housing and education. The final column in the table illustrates that these "benefits in kind" push the "income" of households in the bottom quintile (20 per cent) of households up by around £3,600. Although such benefits also shift up the income of the top 20 per cent (by around £2,000), this means that the ratio of income of the bottom 20 per cent to that of the top 20 per cent leaps from 14.8 per cent before benefits in kind are taken into account to 26.5 per cent after.

Another way of looking at the same thing is to look at the proportion of post-tax income that benefits in kind represent. For the top 20 per cent of non-retired households this is 21 per cent. For the bottom 20 per cent, 94 per cent (Economic Trends *op cit*, Table H)

Now there are some doubts on how accurate the figures on benefits in kind are – especially because education appears to be "pro-poor" partly because of the treatment of students living away from home (they are excluded). Adjusting for this makes benefits in kind less progressive but does not eliminate them (see "Welfare Benefits in Kind and Income Distribution" Evandrou, Falkingham, Hills and Le Grand, Fiscal Studies 1993). In any case the solution here is surely to do with issues of the funding of higher education.

Overall then, this analysis does suggest that even if the money raising mechanism is non-progressive, the net effect is likely to be strongly redistributive. For someone concerned with such issues it is better to put up indirect taxes – if this is more feasible for whatever reasons – and spend the money wisely, than to sit on one's hands in despair!

Conclusion
Redistribution through the tax system must not be deserted, and we must not give up the fight to re-establish direct tax as a legitimate and fair way of proceeding. However we cannot afford to throw out completely any of the mechanisms that may allow us to achieve more equality, and indirect tax has a role to play.

Additionally, if we really do believe that the use of indirect taxes can influence behaviour in ways we deem appropriate (especially in the green area), then we should not be totally frightened off them simply because the initial incidence of the tax may be regressive.

Appendix II
Summary of modelling of environmental tax reform from around Europe

The European carbon/energy tax

Debate in Europe about green tax reform has been dominated by the European Commission's proposal for the gradual introduction of a carbon/energy tax, covering energy use in the domestic, industrial and commercial and transport sectors. A European Commission paper entitled *The Energy Consequences of the Proposed Carbon/Energy Tax* (European Commission, 1992a) suggests that a carbon/energy tax phased in at $3 dollars per barrel of oil equivalent and rising to $10 dollars would reduce energy consumption by 2.8 per cent after seven years. The biggest impact would be on industrial demand, which would fall by 4.8 per cent.

The European Commission's paper *Taxation, Social Security Systems and the Environment* (European Commission, 1993a) summarises internal research which models the economic effects of a 1 per cent general reduction in employers' social security contributions, financed by a CO_2/Energy tax. After 7 years:

● GDP is up 1 per cent

● Employment is up 1 per cent

● The current balance is down 0.1 per cent

● Investment is down 0.2 per cent (though up 0.5 per cent after first year)

● The Consumer Price Index is down 0.7 per cent

The picture which emerges from these and other studies is that tax reform would have a positive impact on employment and growth, an uncertain but small impact on inflation, and a very minor deterioration in the current account balance.

The Commission study also looked at the impact of targeting the cuts in employers' contributions to the low paid. This leads to more positive employment benefits: employment rises by 2.2 per cent rather than 1 per cent. Using the revenue saved due to the drop in unemployment to make further cuts in social security taxes leads to an increase in employment of 3 per cent – 6.6 million extra jobs across the Community.

Alternatives to increasing energy prices.

Assuming it is desirable to reduce employers' social security contributions, is energy taxation the best way to raise the revenue instead? The European Commission has looked into this, too. It concludes that higher income tax would be a viable option, boosting employment less than in the energy tax scenario, but with a positive impact on inflation. (The main problem with higher income tax, of course, would be the political impact.) Increasing the rate of VAT depresses demand and thus the package has no net impact on employment. Moreover, inflation goes up and economic growth declines (European Commission, 1993a).

The DRI study

The impact of a broader tax reform package, including a carbon/energy taxes, higher transport taxes, agricultural input taxes and water taxes as well as a range of non-fiscal measures, has been modelled for the European Commission by a consortium of consultants led by DRI. They predict that:

● GDP is 1 per cent higher in 2010 than in reference case.

● There is a shift away from agriculture and energy, and towards both manufacturing and services.

● If Employers' Social Security Costs are reduced, there is an increase in employment of 2.2 million by 2010, reducing the unemployment rate by 1 per cent.

● Inflation is higher, due to internalisation of transport and energy costs into price of goods. (DRI, 1994)

National studies

It would clearly be better to implement reform right across the EU. But national jealousies over taxation make this unlikely – fiscal matters are explicitly excluded from the operation of qualified majority voting which applies to most environmental policy. There have therefore been a number of studies modelling the impact for individual member states. The impact of the carbon/energy tax plus reductions in employers social security contributions on six member states is modelled in a paper presented at an OECD conference in 1994. This predicts effects on employment and GDP in 2001 shown in the table below.

Table AII.1 Effects on employment and GDP in 2001

	Employment	GDP
GERMANY	↑ 0.79%	↑ 0.22%
FRANCE	↑ 0.44%	↑ 0.04%
UK	↑ 0.56%	↓ 0.42%
ITALY	↑ 0.79%	↑ 0.72%
NETHERLANDS	↑ 0.3%	↓ 0.16%
BELGIUM	↑ 0.88%	↑ 0.57%

(Majocchi, 1994)

There have also been a number of national studies, some of which are summarised below.

The UK

A study by Cambridge Econometrics looks at the impact of the carbon/energy tax, combined with increased spending on energy efficiency programmes and reductions in employers' national insurance. It suggests that as well as the 13 per cent reduction in CO_2 emissions, there would be a net increase in employment of 278,000 and a slight increase in the rate of economic growth. Inflation would be marginally higher, and the balance of payments would deteriorate.

The paper also models the effects of using the revenues from the fuel escalator to reduce employers' national insurance contributions. This leads to an increase in employment of 191,000. Finally, the effects of a fuel escalator of 17.5 per cent per year are calculated, with the revenue being used first to eliminate employers' NICs and then to provide wage subsidies. Not surprisingly, the impact on employment is substantially greater, with 1.3 million extra jobs. Growth increases, inflation is down and the balance of payments improves due to a reduction in oil imports.

Germany

The Deutsches Institut fur Wirtschaftung carried out a study into the impact of a unilateral tax reform in Germany, involving progressively rising energy taxes leading after ten years to a 24 per cent increase in the price of petrol, a 46 per cent increase for household electricity and a 96 per cent increase for industrial electricity. There would be an increase in employment of 600,000, and insignificant impacts on economic growth and competitiveness. Energy use declines by 7 per cent (DIW, 1994).

France

A study by Erasme modelled the impact of a carbon/energy tax, with the receipts used for: financial incentives towards energy conservation, for both households and industry (16 per cent of total receipts); lowering VAT on non-energy intensive goods (53 per cent); lowering employers' national insurance (31 per cent). This is regarded as having the best macro-economic and environmental effect, reducing carbon dioxide emissions by 13.4 per cent and creating 90,000 new jobs (Erasme, 1994).

Sectoral impacts

The DRI study for the European Commission, models the impact in terms of average annual growth on different manufacturing sectors of two scenarios: policies in the pipeline (PIP) which includes a carbon/energy tax; and policy integration (INT) which includes a broad range of environmental taxes and offsetting reductions in labour taxes. For only one sector, ores and metals, will there be an actual contraction (and this occurs in the referance scenarios too). Sectors where the policy integration scenario would cause a lower growth rate include transport equipment, food, drink and tobacco, textiles and clothing and pulp and paper. This is because their prices are increased by the internalisation of environmental costs. Sectors which gain under policy integration are those which supply the advanced the advanced materials which will be in higher demand, including non-metallic minerals, rubber and plastics processing and metal processing (DRI, 1994).

Table AII.2 Change in Production Growth By Sector in Manufacturing PIP and INT vs REF
(Difference in Average Annual Growth Rates over the Period 1992 to 2010)

	PIP	INT
Ores and metals	-0.07	-0.37
Non-metallic minerals	-0.03	+1.43
Chemicals	-0.04	+0.00
Metal Products	-0.06	+0.61
Mechanical engineering	+0.03	+0.00
Office and EDP	-0.02	-0.06
Electrical equipment	-0.03	-0.12
Transport equipment	-0.05	-0.37
Food, drink and tobacco	+0.05	-0.12
Textiles and clothing	+0.01	-0.21
Pulp, paper and printing	-0.02	-0.21
Miscellaneous products	-0.07	-0.22
Rubber and plastics processing	-0.05	+1.35
Manufacturing total	**-0.02**	**+0.06**

Source: DRI

The next table, from the Bureau du Plan – Erasme (1993) study, shows the impact of cuts in employers' social security cuts, financed by a carbon/energy tax, on broad sectors in six countries. This suggests that only in the energy sector will there be a net reduction in employment, and even here the negative impact will be small. The new jobs are fairly evenly distributed between manufacturing and services, except in Italy where services will create 90,000 new jobs.

Table AIII.3 Sectorial Employment and GDP Growth for the Six Countries in 2001
(Differences in thousands to the baseline)

	DB	FR	UK	IT	NL	BE	EUR-6
Total employment	234.7	98.8	150.1	165.6	15.2	32.5	696.9
Total employment	0.79	0.44	0.56	0.79	0.30	0.88	0.64
Energy sector	-0.7	-0.6	0.7	0.0	-0.4	-0.4	-1.5
Industry	70.9	40.8	69.1	24.4	3.1	9.9	218.2
intermediate goods	20.1	11.23	11.7	5.7	0.8	2.7	52.2
investment goods	31.9	9.0	44.5	8.5	0.2	1.6	95.7
consumption goods	18.9	20.6	12.9	10.2	2.1	5.6	70.3
Building sector	48.1	10.2	9.2	8.3	2.4	2.1	80.3
Transport	26.2	5.1	21.1	17.7	2.2	4.7	76.9
Sevices	76.4	43.4	43.3	90.9	7.9	15.9	277.9
GDP	**0.22**	**0.04**	**-0.42**	**0.72**	**-0.16**	**0.57**	**0.15**

References

Arden Clark C (1994) *Environmental Taxes and Charges and Border Tax Adjustment – GATT rules and energy taxes* WWF Gland.

Barrett M (1994) *Aircraft pollution Environmental Impacts and Future Solutions* WWF Gland.

Bate R & Morris J (1994) *Global Warming: apocalypse or hot air?* IEA London.

Beckerman W (1975) *Pricing for Pollution* IEA London.

Bradshaw J (1993) *Household budgets and living standards* Joseph Rowntree Foundation York.

British Petroleum (1983) *Statistical review of world energy* BP London.

British Petroleum (1995) *Economic Instruments for Environmental Protection* BP London.

British Social Attitudes (1992) *The North Report* SCPR Dartmouth Aldershot.

Bureau du Plan – Erasme (1993) *Un redéploiement fiscal au service de l'emploi* Brussels.

BCSD – Business Council for Sustainable Development (1994) *Internalizing Environmental Costs to Promote Eco-Efficiency* Geneva.

Cameron J, Demaret P & Geradin D (1994) *Trade and the Environment: the search for balance* Cameron & May, London.

CBI (1995) *Moving Forward: a business strategy for transport* CBI.

Commission on Social Justice (1994) *Social Justice; strategies for national renewal* Vintage/IPPR.

Convery F & Rooney S (1996) *Making markets work for the economy and the environment – lessons from experience in Greece, Ireland, Portugal and Spain* Paper presented to European Foundation workshop February.

Corry D, Hewett C & Tindale S (1996) *Energy '98: competing for power* IPPR.

Crombie H (1994) *Sustainable Development and Health* Public Health Trust Birmingham.

Coopers & Lybrand (1993) *Landfill costs and prices: correcting possible market distortions* HMSO.

DIW – Deutsches Institut fur Wirtschaftsforschung (1994) *The economic effects of ecological tax reform* Berlin.

DoE (1990) *This Common Inheritance.* White Paper on the Environment HMSO.

DoE (1994a) *Sustainable Development: the UK strategy* HMSO.

DoE (1994b) *Mineral Planning Guidence 6* HMSO.

DoE (1996a) *Review of the potential effects of climate change in the United Kingdom* HMSO.

DoE (1996b) *Air Quality Strategy* Consultation Paper HMSO London.

DTI (1995) *Energy Projections for the UK: energy use and energy-related emissions of carbon dioxide in the UK 1995-2020* (Energy paper 65) HMSO.

DGB (1995) *Vorschlag fur eine Energiesteuer* Dusseldorf.

DRI (1994) *The potential benefits of integration of environmental and economic policies; an incentive-based approach to policy integration* CE Brussels.

ECOTEC (1991) *Review of the sensitivity of demand for primary aggregates to environmental costs* Birmingham.

Employment Policy Institute (1996) *Memorandum to House of Commons Education and Employment Committee Inquiry into Social Costs and their Effects on Employment* London.

European Commission (1992a) *The energy consequences of the proposed carbon/energy tax* CEC Brussels.

European Commission (1992b) *The climate challenge. Economic aspects of the Community's strategy for limiting CO_2 emissions* European Economy 51 Brussels.

European Commission (1993a) *Taxation, social security systems and environment: fiscal reform for more employment* CEC Brussels.

European Commission (1993b) *Growth, competitiveness and employment; the challenges and ways forward into the 21st century* CEC Brussels.

European Commission (1996) untitled paper 487 final, 20 March.

Eyre N (1996) "Meeting environmental objectives in liberalised energy markets" in Corry *et al, op cit.*

Godlee F &Walker A (1992) "Health and the Environment" *BMJ* London.

Goodwin P (1992) "A review of new demand elasticities with special reference to short and long run price effects of price changes" *Journal of Transport Economics and Policy London*, May.

Hewitt P (1989) *A Cleaner, Faster London* IPPR.

Hillman M & Plowden S (1996) *Speed control and transport policy* PSI.

Hills, J (1996) "Tax Policy: are there still choices?" in Halpern *et al* (ed) *Options for Britain: a strategic policy review*, Dartmouth Aldershot.

Hoeller P & Coppel L (1992) "Carbon taxes and current energy policies in OECD countries" in *Economic Studies 19*, special issue on "The economics of Reducing CO_2 emissions", OECD, Paris.

Holtham G & Mayhew K (1996) *Tackling Long Term Unemployment* IPPR.

Howarth D, Nikitopolous P and Yohe G (1989) *On the ability of carbon taxes to fend off global warming* mimeo.

Hutton S & Hardman G (1993) *Assessing the impact of VAT on fuel on low income households: analysis of the fuel expenditure date from the 1991 family expenditure survey* Social Policy Research Unit University of York.

International Energy Agency – IEA (1994) *World Energy Outlook* OECD/IEA Paris.

International Monetary Fund (1994) *Tax policy and the environment: theory and practice* IMF Washington.

Jackman R, Layard R & Nickell S (1996) "Combatting unemployment: is flexibility enough?" Paper presented to OECD Conference on Interactions between structural reforms, macroeconomic policies and economic performance, January.

Jacobs M (1990) *Sustainable Development: greening the economy* Fabian Society.

Jacobs M (1996) *The Politics of the Real World* Earthscan London.

Johnson P McKay S & Smith S (1990) "The distributional consequences of environmental taxes" *IFS Commentary 23* Institute for Fiscal Studies.

Lansley S & Gowan D (1994) *Fair Taxes* Campaign for Fair Taxation London.

Lufthansa (1995) *Umweltbericht 1994* Frankfurt.

Mabey (1995) *Macroeconomic modelling of carbon taxes* London Business School.

Majocchi A (1994) *The employment effects of eco-taxes; a review of empirical models and results* OECD.

Meade J (1988) *Agathopia: the economics of partnership* Aberdeen University Press/David Hume Institute.

Morton AC (1979) ed. *Political writings of William Morris* Lawrence & Wishart.

Moore & Hanton (1995) Company Cars *Transport 2000* London.

Mulgan G & Murray R (1993) *Reconnecting Taxation* Demos London.

Nickell S & Bell B (1995) "The collpase of demand for the unskilled and unemployment across the OECD" in *Oxford Review of Economic Policy* February.

OECD (1992) *Climate Change: designing a practical tax system.*

OECD (1993a) *Environmental policies and industrial competitiveness.*

OECD (1993b) *Taxation and the Environment: complementary policies.*

OECD (1995) *Report on Trade and the Environment to the OECD Council at Ministerial Level.*

Opschoor J & Voss H (1989) *Economic Instruments for Environmental Protection* OECD Paris.

Owens S, Anderson V & Brunskill I (1990) *Green Taxes: a budget memorandum* IPPR.

Parker M (1994) *The Politics of Coal's Decline* RIIA London.

Paxton A (1994) *The Food Miles Report* SAFE Alliance London.

Pearce D, Markandya A & Barbier E (1989) *Blueprint for a Green Economy* Earthscan London.

Pearson M & Smith S (1990) *Taxtaion and Environmental Policy: some initial evidence* IFS, London.

Pigou A (1920) *The Economics of Welfare.* Macmillan, London.

Plowden S & Hillman M (1996) *Speed Control and Transport Policy* PSI London.

Ponting C (1991) *A green history of the world* Penguin London.

Pototschnig A (1996) *Experience with air pollution charges in Poland* Paper presented at European Foundation workshop, February.

Repetto R (1992) *Green Fees: how a tax shift can work for the environment and the economy* WRI Washington.

Royal Commission on Environmental Pollution (1994) *18th Report; Transport and the Environment.*

Smith S & Pearson M (1991) *The European carbon energy tax proposal* IFS.

Smith S (1995) *Green Taxes and Charges: policy and practice in Britain and Germany* IFS London.

Sterner T (1994) "Environmental Tax Reform: the Swedish Experience" *Studies in Environmental Economics and Development* Goteborg University.

Swedish Ministry of the Environment (1996) *The Swedish Experience: taxes and charges in environmental policy* Stockholm.

Taylor R (1992) *The Market in Environment* Adam Smith Institute.

TemaNord (1994) *The use of economic instruments in Nordic environmental policy* Nordic Council of Ministers Copenhagen.

Transport 2000 (1995) *Moving Together: policies to cut car commuting* T2000 London.

Treasury (1996) *Subsidies and the Environment* Paper for the Government Panel on Sustainable Development HMSO.

Von Weizacker E (1994) *Earth Politics* Zed Books London and New Jersey.

Von Weizacker E & Jesinghaus J (1992) *Ecological tax reform: a policy proposal for sustainable development* Zed Books London and New Jersey.

Wallis K (1991) "Leaking Gas in the Greenhouse" *Nature* vol 354.

Weiner J (1992) "The Comprehensive Approach, Greenhouse Taxes and Informal Emissions Trading" in *Climate Change: designing a practical tax system* OECD (1992).

World Energy Council (1991) Energy for tomorrow's world quoted in Royal Commission on Environmental Pollution, *op cit*.